People are saying

To say Mike DeClue saved my life probably is too melodramatic to be believed, even if it's true. But to say he helped give me back my life is a perfectly defensible statement. I have witnesses; I have journals; I have a refreshingly successful second marriage. Lots of people listen, Mike understands.

N. Paul Dusseault

You shared many insights about emotional passages, confronting the past, healing and moving forward. You helped me and many others to overcome feelings of fear, loneliness, inferiority, and guilt. I value and trust you as a friend and spiritual leader.

Amy A. Sherrer

I will always remember how Mike helped me in one of my most desperate hours. His inspiration and insight have helped to guide me since then and will into the future.

Collin M. Ohms

Mike helped me understand my feelings regarding specific issues which gave me the courage to move onto a new chapter and a new beginning in my life.

Linda Sloss

Through Mike's listening, he gave me food for thought. At times the food was difficult to swallow, but it helped me get through a very difficult time in my life. I am grateful to Mike and his leadership. I now have a new life of peace, contentment, and happiness.

Wendy Bush

Mike was an excellent counselor to me during a crazy time of my life. My depression is gone and I like myself again. I have developed excellent communication skills and met a wonderful woman. I'm enjoying life again much sooner than I expected.

Rich Stratmann

I feel strongly that Mike assisted me in closing a door to my past and opening a door to a brighter future. His expertise, insight and wisdom helped me make the steps to my healing process.

Ellen A. Levinson

You were important in helping me to get started on the journey to healing. You pushed me to confront my contributions to the problems in my marriage. Though this was difficult and painful, I needed the push. Your courageous honesty and insight enabled me to see how destructive my own insecurities and lack of self-esteem had become to me, him, and our relationship. I still struggle with feelings of hurt and anger but I now know how to forgive and let go.

Mary Anne Rudloff

You gave of your talents beyond what I expected. With your help, I was able to turn my life around and deal with the problems I had denied and hidden. My life today is focused in a positive direction thanks to your insight and listening skills.

John Pullmann

Your honesty with your own life experience, both good and bad, inspired me to honestly look at myself and progress from a low spot in my life.

Nancy Raben

Secrets

OF LOVE AND MARRIAGE

by

Michael W. DeClue

Newjoy Press
Ventura, California 93006
United States of America

Secrets
of Love and Marriage

by Michael W. Declue

Published by:
 Newjoy Press
 PO Box 3437
 Ventura, California U.S.A.
 800-876-1373

© Copyright 2000 Michael W. DeClue
Publish Date: January 3, 2001
Printed in the United States of America

Library of Congress Catalog Data

DeClue, Michael W.
Secrets of Love and Marriage
1. Love, marriage
2. Marriage, secrets of love in
3. Relationships, marital and cohabitation

LCCN: 99-80092

ISBN: 1-879899-21-3 $15.95

Dedication

This book is dedicated
to my loving wife, Julia

TABLE OF CONTENTS

PART ONE
The Perfect Principles of Love and Marriage

Secret

PART TWO
The Painful Problems of Love and Marriage

Secret

PART THREE
The Patient Practice of Love and Marriage

FOREWORD

Divorce is one of the fastest growing marital status categories in today's world—in 1970 there were 4.3 million divorces; in 1994, there were 17.4 million.

Statistics related to marriage, relationships, families and children are discouraging—to say the least. Today, the nuclear family represents only 7 percent of the total population. Three thousand kids a day witness their parents' divorce, two parent families account for only 36% of all family households, 40% of children go to bed in a home without a father present, 4.7 million children live with a grandparent, and there are 3.5 million unmarried couple households—seven times more than the number of unmarried couple households in 1970. Every day in America, 40 teenage girls are giving birth to their *third* child.

The U.S. Census Bureau data paints a bleak picture of the traditional two-parent family. All the positive indicators of healthy family life are in sharp decline. (Positive indicators include first time married, children born to married mothers, children living with two parents, family size and fertility rates.)

Is there any hope? "Yes," states Michael W. DeClue, author of *Secrets of Love and Marriage.* Hundreds of books have been written on marriage and relationships but seldom does one find a book written with the personal experiences of Mr. DeClue. He has experienced two divorces, and he is a recovering alcoholic who has been active in the 12-Step recovery program of Alcoholics Anonymous for many years. He and his third wife have been married since 1988. They have two daughters, Natalie, age five, and Nicole, age eight.

In addition, he also brings a wealth of information

gathered in his eight years of work with divorce recovery groups. He has worked with hundreds of men and women who have experienced divorce. My son was one of those touched by him.

I recommend Michael DeClue's book, *Secrets of Love and Marriage*. The book has forty-nine secrets, subdivided into three sections entitled, The Perfect Principals of Love and Marriage, The Painful Problems of Love and Marriage, and The Patient Practice of Love and Marriage.

What are you waiting for? Read *Secrets of Love and Marriage*. Get ready to be encouraged and equipped to grow in your relationship with the one you love.

Kay L. Meyer
Founder and President
Family Shield Ministries, Inc.

ABOUT THE AUTHOR

Michael DeClue holds a degree in Bible and Pastoral Studies from North Central College in Minneapolis, MN, and a Bachelor of Science Degree in Business Administration from the University of Missouri in St. Louis.

His lengthy affiliation as group facilitator and board member of a not-for-profit divorce recovery program have given him the background and experience to write a book that pinpoints the trouble spots and identifies the major causes of most marital problems.

In addition, the author's personal experiences with 12-Step groups such as Alcoholics Anonymous, Al-Anon and Adult Children of Alcoholics enables him to lend personal, spiritual and pragmatic answers to serious relationship issues.

His personal experiences with marriage and divorce give his writing empathic insight. Divorced twice and then married for the third time, he decided to discover the secrets of a good marriage for himself. He embarked on a journey to the past to examine his mistakes, relive the heartache, and remember the pain. What he discovered is not only deeply personal, it is profoundly universal.

The secrets he shares with you in this book have given him a happy marriage and two healthy children. Now the secrets of love and marriage can be your secrets, too. As you read them, you will discover what Michael did—your higher self, a self that will empower you to live happily ever after.

DISCLAIMER

This book is designed to provide information concerning the subject matter covered. It is sold with the understanding that the publisher and author are not engaged in rendering professional counseling services by means of this book

Every effort has been made to make this book as complete and accurate as possible. However, there may be mistakes both typographical and in content. Therefore, this text should be used only as a general guide and not as the ultimate source of information. Furthermore, this book contains information only up to the printing date.

The author addresses relational and marital issues by means of anecdotes. The stories are creations of the author for illustrative purposes only. Any resemblance to specific individuals, living or dead, or to any event, is purely coincidental.

The purpose of this book is to educate and entertain. The author and Newjoy Press shall have neither liability nor responsibility to any person or entity with respect to any loss or damage caused, or alleged to be caused, directly or indirectly, by the information contained in this book.

If you do not wish to be bound by the above, you may return this book to the publisher for a full refund.

INTRODUCTION

Secrets of Love and Marriage uses spiritual truths, 12-Step recovery techniques, practical advice and timely examples to give you meaningful solutions to the relationship riddle.

The book contains references to my own experience with marriage and divorce. It contains insights gained in my work with a divorce recovery program and my affiliations with 12-Step groups. Given this background and the rate of divorce and separation in marriages in this country and others, I decided to share what I learned with other seekers of truth.

I have no doubt that untold millions want successful marriages or relationships but know little about how to make their dreams a reality. They struggle with problems they never knew existed and end up divorced, separated, alone and lonely. They feel confused and ready to give up in their quest for a successful marriage or relationship.

These are the people I originally had in mind when I decided to write this book. However, much to my surprise, I discovered another group of seekers—couples in a relationship or marriage who have lost the spark of enthusiasm and intimacy. They too suffer from feelings of loneliness and despair. Their problems are similar to the problems experienced by my initial audience.

Thus, it is for seekers everywhere, whether in or out of a relationship, that I have written this book.

To help you on your journey through the *Secrets of Love and Marriage*, the book is divided into three parts:

Part I identifies the perfect principles of love and marriage. All of you know what you would want if you were able to design a relationship for yourselves. Whether your ideals are practical or not has little importance, they represent your highest desires and therefore they become your ultimate aim in life. Ideals are what dreams are made of. They are the essence of hope, and the spirit that motivates people to attempt a relationship or marriage in the first place.

When you see your cherished ideals operative in others, if only for a moment, you know you can have what others have if only you could get it right.

Part II exposes the painful problems people encounter with love and marriage.

If obstacles prevent you from achieving what you want in a relationship or marriage, then surely there must be a way to identify them and understand their origin. After all, how else can you remove these nagging impediments and continue your quest for the best life has to offer.

In this section, I name the demons by unmasking major character defects and examining their root cause. Self knowledge is the first step in freeing oneself from destructive behavior and experiencing positive results. However, this knowledge must be *used* in a way that will help achieve the relationship or marriage for which you have been searching.

Part III offers practical solutions to help make your marriage or relationship enjoyable and rewarding.

Too many times trial and error is used when trying to figure out what course to take in a given situation. This causes reactions harmful to our relationship or marriage. Sometimes, people seek out advisers or relationship gurus for answers, or take the advice of someone else and do what they would do. This too, can cause further damage to a relationship.

In this last section, I give practical solutions that work. They are founded on patience, understanding and a nonjudgmental spirit that depart from the destructive tendency to value judge yourselves or others.

Part three is the third and final leg of the journey through the *Secrets of Love and Marriage*. It is a journey that will lead you to the ultimate goal—a satisfactory relationship with your loved one and with your highest self.

Enjoy the journey, reap the rewards.

Part One

The Perfect Principles of Love & Marriage

Secret One
A PRESCRIPTION FOR HAPPINESS

Have you ever wished someone would write a prescription for your ailing relationship or marriage, one that would inject it with enough happiness for the two of you? Sure you have. Everyone has from time to time.

No doubt you've read numerous books, periodicals, magazines and manuals, hoping to find the magic potion. Maybe you've gone to therapists, clergy, psychiatrists and counselors for answers only to leave feeling discouraged and ready to give up.

Here is good news. A prescription exists that will make your relationship or marriage happy again. Take a *loving* attitude and mix it with lots of *romance* and watch your relationship or marriage spring back to life.

I'll begin with the idea of a loving attitude to make sure you understand my secret elixir.

Typically, when you use the word "loving" to describe someone, you think of a genuinely warm, thoughtful person who looks for opportunities to express love. He knows actions speak louder than words and love must be shown, not merely talked or thought about.

I recall a story told to me by a friend of mine that beautifully illustrates the point. He said his father passed away shortly before his fifth birthday. When he turned eight, his mother remarried. Suddenly, he found himself living with a stepfather.

Understandably, he felt frightened. "Will our stepfather love us? Will we love him? Will he provide for us, protect us and treat us like his own?"

The answers became clear within days.

First, his stepfather made sure their house was in good

repair and that his new wife and family had plenty of food on the table and clothes to wear. Next, he taught my friend how to ride a bike, fly a kite and hit a baseball. He showed my friend's sister how to play hop scotch, square dance and make a yo-yo do incredible things.

As summer approached, my friend's stepfather signed him up for little league and put aside money each week so that my friend's sister could take swimming lessons. He even bought mother a car and took his new family on their first vacation.

When my friend decided to go to college, his stepfather paid for his tuition. At his sister's wedding, he walked her down the aisle. When their mother complained that their house would no longer accommodate family and friends on holidays, he bought a bigger one.

To this day, my friend remembers his stepfather as a loving person, someone who went out of his way to offer support and encouragement, and make sure his wife and family knew they were loved.

"But that is not me," you say. You don't feel loving and your attitude reflects it. For you, love has become a lifeless noun, a baffling enigma and a nearly incomprehensible term. Maybe you have convinced yourself you have to feel loved before you can love someone.

Perhaps you believe, as many do, that love will find you when you are not looking for it, or maybe you believe you have been searching in all the wrong places.

Surprise! Love can only be experienced by loving someone. Don't wait for someone to love you. Love was meant to be enlivened by activity, not wasted by neglectful passivity. Unless a charitable act or compassionate deed inspires this otherwise inanimate expression, love will remain dormant, the victim of inertia.

Why not transform your concept of love from an ordinary noun into an active verb. Like my friend's stepfather, you too, will be remembered as a loving person.

Romance represents the second important ingredient in my prescription for happiness. Plenty of romance combined with a loving attitude works wonders. It saddens me that so few know so little about the concept of romance and what this beautiful term really means.

First and foremost, romance requires spontaneity. Spontaneity is the invisible force that makes romance seem vibrant and alive, never dull or boring, but forever youthful and growing.

"But how does spontaneity work?" you may ask. One of the most spontaneous moments of my married life happened one dreary Friday in November. Another week was drawing to a close and my wife and I were experiencing the blahs. Suddenly, I had a wonderful idea. Without hesitation, I picked up the phone and called my wife.

"Let's spend the weekend away, just the two of us," I suggested.

"Throw some things together and we'll leave as soon as I get home," I exclaimed with new found excitement.

I hung up the phone, then fear struck. "Does she think I've lost my mind? Did I sound too impulsive? Is she rethinking my idea? Will she reject it? Will I feel rejected if she does?" These were the thoughts playing on my mind as I left my office and hurried home.

To my delight, my wife was inspired by my suggestion. When I arrived at our door, the bags were packed and off we went for a romantic weekend together.

The neatest part of the experience was that my wife didn't think I had lost my mind or that my idea was weird. She loved it.

I loved her for loving my idea.

The secret to spontaneity is that it is simply freedom of self expression without fear of negative repercussions. Spontaneity will only flourish in a nonjudgmental environment. This is the underlying beauty of this captivating concept.

Spontaneity relies on an active imagination. A healthy imagination provides the creative spark that awakens the romantic's spontaneous spirit. Then the person uses their imagination to inspire their spouse or loved one in extraordinary ways.

The key to activating your imaginative genius is to be open to the many possibilities for improving your relationship or marriage, and concentrating on what's right about your spouse or loved one. Unfortunately, too many people use their imagination in a negative way and fail to seize opportunities to make things right.

A romantic accentuates the positive and looks for ways to deepen their relationship with their spouse or loved one. In so doing, they inoculate themselves against the dreaded "disease" of discontentment.

It may surprise you, but most people consider themselves romantic—even though millions of hearts are broken each year.

You are probably familiar with those who use romance to "conquer" the other person. When they get what they want, they lose interest and move on in search of another "conquest." These are people who think only of themselves and what they can get.

Not so with a true romantic. They are spendthrifts who are always in the red. Not in terms of financial accounts, but in thoughtful deeds and acts of kindness. An unselfish attitude transforms an ordinary person into a true romantic.

Go ahead. Mix a loving attitude with plenty of romance. No doubt it's the medicine your relationship or marriage needs. Apply it in liberal doses and you'll find the prescription for happiness for which you have been searching. That's a promise!

Secret Two
THE AWESOME POWER OF INTIMACY

Love possesses secret transforming properties only operational through the awesome power of intimacy. But first you must forsake all others before you can become one with another.

Forsaking all others can be a scary proposition. I remember those anxious hours before the wedding when I suddenly realized I wouldn't be going home to mom and dad, the two people with whom I felt the safest. Frightened, I began thinking about my options. Should I go through with it? How could I bow out now? What would happen if I did?

Although scared out of my wits, I summoned enough courage to charge down the aisle of matrimony without an inkling of what I was in for and without understanding the least thing about the concept of intimacy.

Why all the anxiety? Looking back, I know I was petrified by the idea of living with another person and letting that person in on the real me. Although the other person was my wife, I thought the closer she got, the higher the probability she might see my inferiority and leave. I felt that was a risk I couldn't afford to take. Instead of forsaking all others, I secretly continued to cling to my father and mother.

My young bride was also emotionally challenged by the prospects of living with another person. Neither of us would allow the other into our private world. After living emotionally apart for nearly five years, our marriage ended in divorce.

Obviously, a certain degree of maturity is essential to a successful marriage. A couple must be willing to forsake

7

family and friends to build a life together. Yet, finding intimacy with each other will prove to be a formidable challenge to any couple.

Why is intimacy so difficult to achieve? As a prerequisite to intimacy, two people must make the decision that they will allow each other in on their innermost secrets. A decree of this magnitude demands that you drop your facade and say, "Here I am. This is the real me."

It took another 15 years and another failed marriage before I finally understood the power of intimacy. I stumbled onto it on my third date with Julia. (I didn't know it then, but we would eventually marry and have two beautiful daughters together.)

On this occasion we were seated at a posh restaurant and a waiter came by with the wine list. After nervously reviewing the various wines that were available I sheepishly turned to the waiter and order iced tea. Julia quickly followed by asking for a cola. I glanced around the room and observed well-dressed couples sipping champagne and sampling exotic drinks. Feeling self-conscious, I turned to Julia and our eyes met. Neither of us said a word for several moments. Then, inexplicably, I felt the need to open up—to reveal who I really am.

I began awkwardly, stumbling over my words at first as I explained to Julia why I had declined the wine list. It wasn't long, however, before I heard myself telling her about my 12-step program. I explained how alcoholism played a role in destroying two previous marriages and why I sought help. I assured her I wasn't proud of my past but that I had learned some valuable lessons.

I also revealed to Julia how, after high school, I entered college to study for the ministry and how my plans were ended by my first divorce and by alcoholism. This was particularly difficult to talk about but Julia listened as I continued to talk—leaving no stone unturned. Then, with the final revelation I sat back and quietly waited for her response.

I have to admit. I was prepared for the worst. What happened was more than I hoped for. Julia looked into my eyes and said, "I admire you for what you're doing. It takes a tremendous amount of courage to ask for help and try and change your life for the better. I'm behind you all the way. Besides, everybody makes mistakes." She then shared some of her own.

Afterwards I could hardly contain myself. I hadn't been rejected. In fact, Julia seemed to like me even more than she did before I revealed my inner self.

Reflecting on the experience later, I realized what I felt was unconditional love and acceptance. This is not only the most beautiful feeling in life but a prerequisite for intimacy.

Since then Julia and I have shared even more. We've explored our strengths and admitted our weaknesses, confessed our doubts, and confronted our fears. We shared memories, both good and bad. However, in spite of these beautiful moments there are plenty of issues to talk about if we hope to achieve an even deeper level of intimacy with each other.

Intimacy is a process. It deepens over time—not over night. Intimacy must be cultivated and nurtured—not repressed or neglected. Intimacy requires a long-term investment—not a one-time contribution. Don't short-change yourself and don't short-change the other person. Take the time. Invest the energy.

Stephen R. Covey, in his national bestselling book, *The 7 Habits of Highly Effective People*, tells of his experience with intimacy.

For a period in his life, he and his wife lived on the island of Laie off the north shore of Oahu, Hawaii. While there, he came up with what he termed a "revolutionary" idea. Every day he would take time away from his busy schedule to lunch with his wife. He would pick her up on his old red Honda 90 trail cycle. They would ride slowly along for about an hour, just talking. They usually found an isolated part of the beach where they parked the Honda and walked about 200 yards to a secluded spot. There they would eat a picnic lunch and continue to talk.

At first they talked about all kinds of topics—people, ideas, events, the children, his writing, their family at home, future plans, and so forth. Over time, little by little, their communication deepened and they began to talk more and more about their inner worlds. They talked about their upbringing, their scripting, their fears, and their self-doubts. As they became intensely immersed in their conversations, they began to observe themselves in them. They discovered how their inner world affected the way they viewed their outer world.

About this experience, Mr. Covey said, "We began an exciting adventure into our interior worlds and found it to be more exciting, more fascinating, more absorbing, more compelling, more filled with discovery and insight than anything we'd ever known in the outside world."

He goes on to say, "Perhaps it doesn't take too much imagination to envision the level of understanding and trust we were able to reach by spending at least two hours a day, every day, for a full year, in deep communication. There were many rich fruits from those months. Our communication became so powerful that we could almost instantly connect with each other's thoughts."

What Stephen Covey and his wife Sandra achieved together was the beauty and wonder of becoming one through the awesome power of intimacy. It began with the decision, or "revolutionary" idea, to risk letting each other in at a deep personal level. For them, it culminated in an experience such as they had never known before.

You don't need to own a trail bike or live on a Hawaiian island to spend quality time together. You don't need to sit on a sunlit beach to share your innermost self. You only need to begin communicating right where you are.

It might take time before you're ready, but if you are not ready, be patient. You will eventually open up. When the time comes the rewards will be indisputable.

Whenever I dare to share my private world with Julia, I inevitably feel acceptance, understanding, love and support such as I've never felt before.

You may be wondering—what if the other person is reluctant to open up? What should I do? The answer is simple—go slow. He or she may need to know if you can be trusted. Things may have occurred in the past that he or she is reluctant to discuss—at least initially. Give time to get the issues out so you can offer unconditional love and acceptance and validate their self-worth.

Stay attentive. Listen but don't judge, editorialize or lecture. Don't try to impose your timetable for processing your partner's issues. When ready, he or she will share.

Remember. The mysterious power of intimacy is a process that begins when two people decide to really get to know each other. Decide, then take your time. You're in for the experience of your life if you do.

Secret Three
SIX KEYS TO A SUCCESSFUL MARRIAGE

Are you happy in your marriage? If so, then count yourself lucky. If not, then maybe you need to explore this secret. You'll discover six keys to a successful marriage. **Key Number One:** Love yourself.

No man or woman ever truly loved another without first loving him or herself. Love who you are and what you are.

Your mother and father had nothing to do with selecting the combination of chromosomes that ultimately decided your physical attributes. Your height, the color of your eyes, the texture of your hair and the nature of your abilities are unique. Your attributes and experience determine your ability to think, to dream, to love, to share, care, and create.

Unfortunately, a large number of people find this simple truth difficult to accept. They feel inferior, inadequate and flawed. In truth, nothing is wrong with them. Thinking you are flawed is guaranteed to undermine your self-esteem.

The story in the bible of the prodigal son gives you a beautiful illustration of whom you are and the trouble you can get into when the concept you have of yourself is faulty. As the story goes, the prodigal son rejected who he was, acted like someone he wasn't and wound up living in conditions that insulted his dignity.

When this wayward lad finally grew sick and tired of residing outside the abundance of his birthright, he gathered himself and scampered back to his father who once again restored him to his rightful position as heir to

12

all that he owned.

Like the prodigal son, many people wind up living beneath their dignity. They feel ashamed of whom they are and strike out in search of something to make themselves feel better. When a person tries to "fix" himself or herself with relationships, sex, alcohol, money, careers or things, he or she eventually finds him or herself living in an emotional or relational pigsty. Self-esteem sinks into despair and hopelessness.

Wise up and realize who you are by turning your focus to the positive part of yourself. Learn to love and appreciate yourself.

Key Number Two: Accept your spouse or loved one just the way they are without trying to change or "fix" them.

It is a psychological truth that people dislike in others the very things they dislike about themselves. Because of this flaw, they tend to criticize their spouses or loved ones.

I recall criticizing Julia for the way she treated our daughter, Nicole, during a period known as the "terrible twos." I thought she should have been more tolerant when Nicole threw her little temper tantrums. Using hindsight, I realized the most trying episodes usually occurred around 5:30 in the evening. Both of us were exhausted from the work day and dinner was our immediate concern—not to mention one of us usually had a commitment we needed to keep later that evening.

In spite of our hectic schedules, I would often wonder, "What is Julia's problem?" Invariably, I would make a comment such as, "Why can't you just ignore Nicole? She'll quiet down eventually." This, of course, made Julia angry. We would find ourselves arguing without either of us really knowing why.

As I began to think about those tension packed evenings, I discovered I shared my wife's frustrations about Nicole's behavior. Somehow, I would deny my feelings as if whatever was going on didn't involve me.

13

I also discovered I was uncomfortable and ashamed of the way I felt about our daughter when she threw her tantrums. However, instead of dealing with my own negative emotions, I chose to deal with Julia's.

Quite naturally, it's easier to take someone else's inventory than it is our own. I stood in judgement of Julia and ignored the same feelings of impatience in myself. I directed my intolerant behavior toward her rather than Nicole.

Since then, I've learned to ask myself questions such as, "What is it about my wife or this situation that annoys me? What feeling or issue did this incident evoke in me that I need to look at? What button is she pushing and why?"

Once I understand the answers to these few questions, I no longer feel the need to judge my wife because the real problem becomes clear. When the problem becomes clear negative reactions disappear.

Key Number Three: Enjoy yourself and the one you love for each of you is unique.

Never has anyone been exactly like either of you. Furthermore, there never will be.

Honor who you are and what you are. Recognize and appreciate all you and your loved one bring to your relationship or marriage. If you do, you'll have truly lived. Developing the special talents, gifts and interests that make you unique is the finest definition of success that I know.

This has been an extremely important concept for me. Stepping out in faith to write this book is my way of honoring my unique abilities.

The first time I told Julia about my plans, I expected her to cast a dissenting vote, but she surprised me. She seemed pleased, even interested. Julia understood that it was something I needed to do for me. In return, I've been encouraging her to sketch and paint again. These are special things she loved to do as an adolescent but neglected as an adult.

Start today to explore your gifts and talents. Encourage your spouse to do the same. You may both be surprised at what you discover.

Key Number Four: Inner satisfaction is a by-product of right living.

You can't buy, rent or borrow this priceless feeling. Inner satisfaction is a function of how you live your life.

Many people seek satisfaction from money, careers and things, to no avail. The simple good news is that satisfaction can be experienced by anyone. The means for attaining it is the same for everyone. It can only be found by living life the "right way."

A child's earliest learning includes the socialization process that creates a conscience. A person's conscience is the means by which they distinguish right from wrong. All you have to do is let it be your guide and you'll experience the satisfaction you've been searching for.

Key Number Five: Make the right choices.

A successful marriage is also determined by the choices we make. I remember making many wrong choices in two previous marriages. There was the choice to escape feelings of inferiority and the fear of abandonment by hiding in the arms of another woman. There was the choice to run from personal problems and responsibilities by picking up the first drink. There was the choice to flee the overwhelming burden of financial debt by spending an evening gambling my hard earned money away at the track. And there was the choice to risk everything for no good reason other than an evening of frivolity and infidelity.

Those choices not only cost me two marriages and several meaningful relationships, but also the esteem of family and friends and, finally, my own self-respect.

Most choices carry far fewer consequences than the choices I made. For example, the choice to ignore your spouse in favor of an evening in front of the TV. Or the choice to pick up the newspaper at the dinner table instead of listening to your spouse talk about his or her day.

You can also choose to spend time working in the yard or immersed in a hobby while neglecting your spouse. The list is endless and most choices seem harmless until they begin to undermine your marriage.

Every choice you make has a price tag. Ask yourself, "What will this choice cost me?" Chances are, you're unwilling to pay the price for a bad choice. Personally, I'm no longer willing to bear the consequences of making a wrong choice.

I am perfectly agreeable to feeling the warmth and contentment that accompany every right choice. The feeling is indescribable and my emotions beg for more.

Get into the habit of choosing wisely. If you do, the future will hold bright promises and countless rewards.

Key Number Six: Remember that no one is perfect so no one makes the right choices always.

Give yourself and your loved one a break. Allow room for tolerance. Every successful relationship or marriage includes plenty of it.

The meaning of tolerance isn't difficult to understand. It simply means you are not trying to impose your will on your spouse or loved ones.

Tolerance also means you are willing to try and understand the other person by putting yourself in their shoes. Ask yourself, "What could be bothering him or her? What could he or she be thinking?"

If these questions fail to help you achieve a greater degree of tolerance, then ask yourself, "How important is the situation? Am I going to allow this incident to jeopardize my marriage or spoil my relationship? Do I really want to exert my will in this matter? What will be the consequence if I do?"

The answers to these few questions will help you

become more tolerant and allow you to experience an inner peace and contentment like never before.

Any of the six keys will improve your marriage in a given situation. However, for the best results, practice them together and you will turn your stumbling blocks into the stepping stones to a successful relationship or marriage.

Secret Four
THE WORD "WEDDING"

The letters in the word wedding provide an acronym. Each letter stands for a significant idea. Putting the ideas together will transform your marriage from an ordinary relationship into a beautiful love affair.

Appropriately enough, the word "wedding" begins with the letter "w" used to spell the most powerful two letter word in the English language—the word "we." Turn the "w" upside down and you have "me."

The person who begins each conversation with me, I, my or mine has missed the power and importance contained in "we."

Me, my, I and mine are not terms of endearment. They are divisive terms that speak of separation and self. "We" denotes solidarity, togetherness, and affiliation. It implies a close association, a kinship possessing extraordinary similarities. We isn't just little, ole me. We presume the presence of at least two. Two have abilities far greater than one.

Two minds focused on a problem, two hands busy at a task, two hearts united as one rally all the positive forces of the universe to their side.

How can a word consisting of only two letters contain so much power? The answer is simple. By myself, I may not be capable of gaining the prize. Tired, alone and emotionally spent, I may entertain thoughts of giving up. In you, I gain the strength and inspiration to carry on. With me and you there is a strong bond. Two cords tightly intertwined form a union—thousands of times stronger than a single strand.

"If "we" represents such a powerful concept, then why

has my marriage fallen on hard times?" you may ask. Although your question may seem reasonable, any blame for your relational problems cannot be imputed to the word "we." It may, however, be chargeable to a shortage of enthusiasm.

Coincidentally, the next letter in the word wedding is "E," and it stands for "enthusiasm." Enthusiasm comes from the Greek words, *en* and *theos*, which means "in God" or "God within."

Enthusiasm is the divine spark that inspires the mind to think and create. People with enthusiasm have found this truth. That is why they are vivacious, active, and often achieve great things.

All of us have the ability to feel enthusiastic. It's as natural as laughing or smiling. You don't have to throw an extravagant party, take a romantic cruise or exchange expensive gifts to drum it up. Look for the spirit of enthusiasm within and allow it to flood your being and fill your soul. You can do it with a song.

"D" is the third and fourth letters in the word wedding. They stand for "Dreamers." Two "Ds" mean room enough for two dreamers in every marriage.

Without a dream your relationship will perish. Each spouse needs a dream to keep love alive, for too still a dream is to kill the dreamer.

What is your dream? Have you stopped pursuing it or is it still a top priority? This question is as important to you as it is to your spouse. If either of you has lost your dream, you have lost a vital part of your personality. Dreams form the catalyst that stirs the emotions, enlivens the soul, produces hope and challenges our faith in each other.

Go ahead and dream. Dream power is the originating force behind every accomplishment that mankind has ever recorded. Encourage your spouse to dream with you. Whatever the human mind can conceive, it can achieve by the power of two and the magic of enthusiasm.

19

The fifth letter in the word wedding is the letter "I." It presents the idea of independence.

Are you surprised that independence has a role in marriage? Many people make the mistake of relinquishing their rights to independence to their spouse. Usually the wife abdicates her rights to her husband but sometimes it's reversed. In the process, one spouse no longer thinks, speaks or acts on their own volition. They lose respect for each other because they lose their identity.

No one likes to be around someone who never has an opinion or an original thought. People who want to be told what to do are leaning, dependent, pathetic souls who become a burden to those around them.

However, those who say what they think and think for themselves have an air about them that is totally alluring. Their independence makes them attractive. They are interesting, provocative and exciting to be with because they are individuals.

Try it. Be yourself. Say what is on your mind. Express your opinions. Develop your talents and go for your dream. Then you will have attained independence.

The next letter in the word wedding is "N." It begins another powerful two-letter word—no. If you can say "no" and mean it, you will experience less frustration and more joy than you ever thought possible.

Although you may not like to admit it, it's sometimes necessary to say "no" to yourself. This may be the single most difficult discipline any person will ever undertake. Saying "no" to yourself may mean letting go of a long-standing behavior or an intensely personal plan. Saying "no" to yourself may mean sacrificing a selfish desire or an inappropriate thought. Finally, saying "no" to yourself may mean placing your spouse before your own interests.

It's also necessary at times to say, "no" to your spouse. This, too, can be difficult, especially if you are haunted by thoughts of rejection and are into people pleasing.

Nevertheless, if you say "yes" when you mean "no," your actions may ultimately betray you.

Saying "no" establishes boundaries, builds self-esteem and engenders respect. Learn to say "no," and you will experience the esteem and admiration you deserve.

The last letter in the word wedding is "G" and it begins the word gratitude. Gratitude is the electricity that lights a relationship and keeps it burning through good times and bad.

When two people are grateful for each other and for what they have together, they possess a power that will help them transcend all of life's circumstances.

Gratitude for each other is a rich and priceless gift. With gratitude, there is no room for comparisons, discontentment, second guessing or regrets. When you are truly grateful for the person you married, you will treat them as a treasure entrusted to your care and your relationship will be a blessing.

Many people have a knack for concentrating on what they don't have. They perceive something is missing in their spouse or marriage. They are the "have nots" who always compare themselves to others.

Gratitude enables you to focus on what you do have. Gratitude is an attitude and attitude is a choice.

Say to yourself, "This is the person who has chosen to share his or her life with me, I will rejoice and be glad." Exhibit an attitude of gratitude in all that you say and do by dwelling on the positive, focusing on the good, and thinking the best about your spouse and your marriage. If you do, you'll experience a multitude of gratitude and marital bliss. Gratitude forms the capstone of any successful relationship.

If your attitude is lukewarm, begin today to practice positive self talk. Tell yourself to be thankful for what you have and the one with whom you have it. Continue this simple exercise for two weeks. It won't be long before gratitude will flood your heart.

As you go through the day, remember the word wedding. It is the one sure acronym you can rely on to make your marriage a success. Who can resist feeling grateful when things are going well?

Secret Five
THE MEANING OF LOVE

Since the beginning of time, love has played on the heartstrings of young and old alike, luring the adoring male away from his father and mother and into the arms of another. Nevertheless, as basic as the migration from single to married life may seem, trouble often follows.

Why would trouble follow this natural life changing process? Because of the way the interpersonal dynamics of courtship and marriage frequently work.

First, the male falls head over heels for a beautiful girl. They date. All goes well. She likes him. After awhile, they fall in love. He asks her to marry him. She accepts. They marry and the male leaves home. He severs himself from his mother's apron strings, but he instinctively replaces her with his wife. Next, he imitates his father by assuming the dominant role as head of the house and majority owner of all he surveys—including his wife.

Meanwhile, the dutiful wife unwittingly plays the roles of surrogate mother and private valet. With the passing of time, she learns to suppress her feelings and opinions in favor of her husband's. His priorities are her priorities, too.

I know first hand that any couple who find themselves in this kind of one-sided relationship rarely exhibit healthy esteem for themselves or each other. What may have started as love is ultimately aborted by the selfish demands of an immature man who falsely assumes his wife is his possession.

I know the dynamics all too well. I have seen it in troubled marriages and heard it described by numerous women standing on the brink of divorce. The pattern is often the same. The question is, can it be corrected?

If love is a man's inducement for leaving mother and

father and uniting with his wife, then where has love gone wrong? If you will allow me to take some liberties, I will examine the letters that comprise the word love. From this, I think you will derive the answers to this relationship riddle for yourself.

Begin with "L," the first letter in the word love. Assume for a moment that it stands for "loan." Although many men may find this concept difficult to comprehend, a husband doesn't own his wife, neither is he in charge of her nor their relationship.

I often forget and say things such as, "She is my wife," and secretly think she "belongs" to me. I'm quickly reminded that nothing in life is really mine. Much like a philanthropist lends a priceless heirloom to a prestigious gallery, my wife is with me for as long as I love, honor and cherish her.

When I forget who is in control, I only need to think back to the circumstances leading to our first date. What good fortune that our paths should cross and how lucky I felt.

If I begin to act like a "big shot," I think about the other relationships that didn't work out. Why did this one succeed and the others fail? The answer is clear. My marriage is a beautiful gift, and it is mine since I recognize I am not the controller. If I hadn't finally realized that fact, I might have gone through divorce for a third time.

If you honestly examine the circumstances surrounding your own marriage, I think you must admit that trying to control another is futile.

The next letter in the word love is "O." Pretend it stands for the word, opportunity. Falling in love is your opportunity to fashion a relationship and marriage that suits both of you. It does not have to be like mother's and father's marriage—or anyone else's. It doesn't have to suit only you or only her. The marital relationship is best when it is designed by both of you for your consensual

24

enjoyment and pleasure.

Your relationship can be one of perfect symmetry, individual choice, and mutual respect. Leave room for personal development, professional achievements, and spiritual growth.

If you want to create a relationship rewarding for both of you, then sit down and start talking. Ask your wife to describe the kind of relationship she wants. Don't try to influence her—just listen. When she has finished, ask her to listen while you describe the kind of relationship you want. Work out your differences. Compromise if necessary. Be willing to give and take. A relationship designed together will last a lifetime. The one you fashion on your own will not.

The third letter in the word love is "V." Assume it stands for the word vitality.

Vitality will add zest to any relationship. Vitality is the fuel that ignites the emotions and heats a relationship to a red-hot glow. No love needs to cool down, no matter how hot it is. Vitality is the spark that will keep it burning through good times and bad.

Perhaps you think you have lost your vitality and you don't know how to regain it. Vitality is often lost when a person becomes attached to a career, the easy chair, the remote control, a hobby, or the newspaper. You begin to neglect your wife and vitality starts to leave like air escaping from a pin-pricked balloon.

Once neglect robs your relationship of vitality, it begins to die. Neither spouse is meeting the other's needs. When the things vital to a relationship are no longer present, trouble comes calling.

If this describes your relationship, here is good news. Regain lost vitality by using any of the following suggestions: First, set aside at least one night a week to spend quality time together. Plan a night at the movies, dinner at a nice restaurant or any activity that will allow just the two of you to be together,

Quality time is time spent together doing things you both enjoy. You'll be pleased with the way you feel afterwards. Vitality will return and your marriage will feel energized again. Isn't that how you spent your time together when you were first dating and didn't it feel invigorating?

Another way to sustain vitality is by encouraging each other to develop your individual talents and gifts. Support each other in attaining personal, professional and spiritual goals.

If you are a husband who expects his wife to suppress her dreams and aspirations in favor of your own, then vitality will always be missing in your marriage. Keep vitality alive by allowing your wife to grow with you. When you acknowledge her as a person, vitality will return. Try it and see for yourself.

My last vitality producing tip is to suggest both of you participate in the household chores and make sure your wife has enough free time for herself. If you think housework is solely your wife's responsibility, vitality will always be lacking in your marriage. When you help with the laundry, the dishes or the kids, you will help your wife rekindle her vitality and she in turn will rekindle yours.

The fourth and final letter of the word love is "E." Assume it stands for the word equality.

The idea of equality may be the most important concept any couple will ever practice in their marriage.

Equality is the assurance that each spouse has input into the decision making process and neither feels slighted nor left out. Equality means each person is getting their needs met and one spouse isn't selfishly neglecting the other.

Are you the type of husband who tries to play "commander-in-chief" at home? Do you make decisions without consulting your wife? Do you give little or no consideration to your wife's feelings and opinions before making personal or professional plans? Are you a husband who cares little for your wife's needs, while making sure your own needs are met?

If you answered "yes," to any of these questions, you can instill equality by reversing field and honestly addressing the questions listed above. I assure you, there's no better place to start.

Protect your relationship by viewing it as a loan and your marriage as an opportunity to fashion a mutually rewarding relationship together. Also remember that vitality is the key to an invigorating romance, and equality is crucial to your success. Build your relationship around these four ideas and you will experience the true meaning of love. And that is a secret you can count on.

Secret Six
ESTABLISH YOUR PRIORITIES

Are there really any successful marriages? You know, the kind made in heaven? If you have your priorities in order, then you're lucky indeed, for you have the kind of marriage everyone is working for. However, if your priorities are confused, then you are probably unhappy and your marriage is plagued by discontent.

What do priorities have to do with marriage, particularly your marriage? Everything.

Take a moment and think of the couples you know who are unhappy. Where do their priorities lie? What do they value most? Do their priorities—the things that really count in their lives—enrich or detract from their marriage? Has a distinguished career or an obsession for prestige, power, money or things diverted their attention from their partner or spouse? Do they seem lonely and afraid? Do they have anyone to confide in, anyone to hold onto, anyone to share life with? In summary, are they seeking the things of this earth, things that eventually turn to dust in one's hands, ashes in one's mouth or rust in one's garage? If so, you can understand why they are scared and lonely.

Think of those you know who are trying to achieve loftier ideals, the kinds that lend meaning to existence, happiness to the heart, and contentment to the soul? These are the goals to seek. They are accessible to everyone if you look in the right places.

Are you seeking power, status, and money or are you seeking happiness and contentment? These last two are the products of a peaceful home, a successful marriage, and healthy, well-adjusted children.

Ask yourself where *your* priorities lie. Think carefully about your answers. While you are doing that I'll share a story about a man named Jeff who made a career his highest priority and neglected his wife and children in the process.

Jeff was employed at a large financial institution in Chicago. He worked there for nearly 15 years, steadily making his way up the corporate ladder. Jeff regularly spent 60 or more hours a week on the job, catering to his superiors' demands and honing his image as the good corporate soldier. To no one's surprise, Jeff's efforts eventually paid dividends and he was appointed to the position of senior vice-president at a time when the rest of the banking industry was downsizing.

With Jeff's new position came additional responsibility, more money and lots of prestige. He became a regular in the senior officers' dining room. He had his own parking space and a secretary. Jeff was in his element. He had finally arrived and he loved it. His sense of importance and self-esteem were never higher.

However, somewhere along the road to success, Jeff's wife began having an affair. Lonely and longing for intimacy, she fell in love with another man. When Jeff found out, he was heartbroken, but it was too late to save his marriage.

Jeff's wife took their two children and moved to an apartment. Shortly afterwards she filed for divorce. Within several months Jeff's marriage was over and his job became the means for paying alimony and child support. Career aspirations had become a thing of the past. Jeff reached the top of the corporate ladder, but he lost his wife and children along the way.

Jeff eventually enrolled in a divorce recovery group. He admitted too routinely keeping long hours at the office and to a need for his superiors' approval. Jeff's bosses demanded a total commitment from senior staff. Anyone who gave less didn't advance in the company.

As Jeff continued to tell his story it became clear that

his desire for success at any cost alienated his wife's affection and destroyed his relationship with his children. To make matters worse, Jeff invested his time and energy in the one place that could do the least bit of good for his emotional and mental well being—his job.

Although you may never reach the top, you may fall prey to the illusion of prestige and power that beckons from the highest point on the corporate ladder. You may place too much importance on status and success, while missing the satisfaction and fulfillment available in a contented marriage and happy home life.

Millions of people feel compelled to spend 60 to 70 hours a week slaving away at the office, trying to emulate the boss instead of spending quality time with their wife and children.

The recent rash of corporate mergers and the threat of downsizing hasn't helped. These situations have created an environment in which workers feel compelled to devote themselves entirely to their careers and move their spouse and family down on their list of priorities. Little wonder the divorce rate is so high and millions of women are frustrated at the prospect of trying to be both mother and father to their children while dad is busily courting the boss.

Although things may look bleak, there is an irony here. Think for a moment about the successful people you know—people who have what you want. Not the material things, but something more. Something you can't put your finger on. Do their priorities guide their choices and direct their actions? How would you define their character? Would you say they have their priorities straight? Of course they do.

This is the secret to be looking for. Truly successful people set their own agenda and determine their own lifestyle. Truly successful people know who they are is in no way related to what they have, what they do, or what others say or think of them. Truly successful people recognize that success is "being," not achieving.

Truly successful people understand that love and respect from their wife or husband and children are the real accomplishments, not gaining the respect and approval of their superiors.

How about you? Would you describe yourself as a success? How would your wife and children describe you? You will find the answer to these two simple questions when you identify your priorities.

If your priorities are like Jeff's, you may be a success at work and a failure at home. In which case, you may need to take another look at what is really important. All truly successful people have discovered this secret.

Secret Seven
THE GREATEST GIFT

As a man, I have often wondered what to give my wife for Christmas, for her birthday, and for our anniversary. Many men have difficulty selecting an appropriate gift for their wife or loved one, and I'm no different—that is until recently.

After years of struggling with gift giving, I have finally discovered the gift that has no equal. It's the best gift any man could ever hope to give his wife.

Here in Secret Seven, you will discover the perfect gift. First I will review the way men give, including their gifts and their motives for giving them.

Contrary to popular opinion, men are good at giving gifts. The reason is simple. Men would rather communicate their love and affection in some tangible way. They instinctively know it requires little emotional investment to give "things."

Think of all the flowers, diamonds, furs, and other expensive gifts given in the name of love. None of them come close to the best gift of all.

No matter how expensive tangible gifts are, you can give something far more valuable. Give yourself! No expensive gift can compare to the gift that has no price.

Compared to giving yourself, diamonds, furs, cars, homes and other gifts are mere substitutes. Anyone can give them. Many men do. However, until a man gives himself unreservedly to his spouse, nothing of real value has been given.

I'm addressing men for good reason. Men are taught from childhood to act tough, to hide their emotions, not to cry and to be strong. Men learn to avoid all that kissy, huggy stuff, so they have difficulty when it comes to giving themselves.

Another reason men find it difficult to give themselves is that of fear. Fear says to a man, "Don't get too close; you might smother me." A man's survival instincts are activated when he feels his emotional and physical space is about to be invaded. The thought of being engulfed by a woman and trapped in a relationship terrifies him, and so men give gifts as a substitute for giving themselves. It's safer that way. They can stand back and watch as the gift gets cuddled and hugged, secretly breathing a sigh of relief at having escaped a close encounter.

A third major reason men find it difficult to give themselves is called immaturity. Most men don't grow out of puberty until about age 45. Others take longer. Some never do.

Men are typically pampered and protected by their mothers as adolescents so they struggle to grow up. Most secretly want a woman who will give them the same tender loving care their mother gave them at home. That is one reason why men want to take all they can out of a relationship without giving anything back—except for gifts, of course.

Men are not entirely at fault. Women know a man is good for a gift. Many women compare their gifts in an effort to measure a man's sincerity and his degree of affection. As a result, men get away with giving "things" without ever being required to give more.

If you are a man and you find yourself identifying with these characteristics, fear not! Giving yourself is the greatest gift that you could ever hope to give your wife. She will never find an exact replica anywhere. The benefit of giving yourself is that there are no duplicates. Your wife will never have to worry about meeting anyone else who has what she has—you.

No one can ever bring to your marriage, relationship or to life itself, the same qualities, talents and temperament you bring. The special something only you have is the very quality your wife found attractive about you in the first place. So why hold back?

Giving yourself will ensure your spouse or loved one won't be disappointed. In light of your unique personality, withholding yourself would mean you will be giving her less than she deserves. Remember? You are the gift money can't buy.

If you're wondering whether you've been giving yourself or substitutes, here is a set of practical questions that will help satisfy your curiosity.

- Have you been giving your wife your time or have you been giving her things, hoping you would not have to give yourself?
- Were you looking for a "caretaker" when you were looking for a wife?
- Is your wife your soul mate or is she at a stalemate because you have been giving her things rather than yourself?

If the answers are frightening, then play the "what if game." What if she really knew you? Would she like you? Would she love you? What if you don't need or want a caretaker? What if your real need is a close, personal relationship with the woman in your life? What if you are being intimidated by an unreasonable fear? What would happen if you found out you have been missing out on the most exciting experience in life because you have been giving gifts rather than yourself?

Why not take a chance and find out? Try an experiment? Invite your wife to a quaint coffee shop, take a drive down a scenic route, or walk together along a beautiful nature trail. Spend time with her. Hold her hand. Give her a hug. Tell your wife what's going on with you. Stop long enough so she can talk while you listen. Give her your attention and your time.

Ask your wife to explain the experience afterwards.

You may discover you have given her the gift that has no price. You will have given her you.

Secret Eight
WHEN I BECAME A MAN

Much has been written concerning the meaning of love. Many definitions have been offered in poetry and prose. A multitude of prophets and philosophers have attempted to explain love's beauty and splendor. When all is said and done, however, the following treatise written by St. Paul around 56 A.D. has long been acclaimed the most excellent discourse on love ever rendered by mortal man.

Paul wrote, "*Love is patient, love is kind. It does not envy, it does not boast, it is not proud. It is not rude, it is not self-seeking, it is not easily angered, it keeps no record of wrongs.*

Love does not delight in base behavior but rejoices in truth. It always protects, always trusts, always hopes, always preserves.

Love never fails. But where there are prophecies, they will cease; where there are tongues, they will be stilled; where there is knowledge, it will pass away. For we know in part and we prophesy in part, but when perfection comes, the imperfect disappears. When I was a child, I talked like a child, I thought like a child, I reasoned like a child. But when I became a man, I put childish ways behind me. Now we see but a poor reflection as in a mirror; then we shall see face to face. Now I know in part; then I shall know fully, even as I am known. And now these three remain: faith, hope and love. But the greatest of these is love."

As romantic as it is, this renowned passage is more than a heart warming dissertation on the virtues of love as evidenced by the phrase, "When I became a man," which lies at the heart of Paul's narrative. Here, the apostle gives us a rare glimpse into the male psyche and what must transpire in a man's attitudes and actions before he can realistically expect to experience love first hand.

Many men have difficulty with relationships because they haven't quite grown up. Immaturity prevents them from loving anyone and they often wind up alone, feeling spurned and rejected without knowing why.

As a prerequisite, love requires patience and kindness, and these are attributes few men possess. The male gender is taught at an early age to get out in the salt mines and out-think, outperform and out maneuver everyone else to eke out a living in a "dog-eat-dog" world.

A man has little patience for anyone standing between him and a goal. That includes a spouse or loved one if he thinks they are preventing him from achieving what he wants. An immature man can be extremely unkind when someone appears to be thwarting his efforts or getting more out of the game of life than he.

Defeating the competition and taking first prize is of paramount importance in the immature male's world. Competition and comparison are the ways in which an immature man derives a sense of superiority. Of course there's always a winner and a loser. This produces envy in the one who feels he has been deprived.

Envy in a male's world can take several forms. He may envy his neighbor for the car he drives, the house he lives in, the clothes he wears, the woman he is married to and the success he seems to be enjoying on the job.

Envy makes a childish man resort to boasting and name dropping which are nothing more than futile attempts at impressing others. He may also exhibit rude or caustic behavior, another sign his ego has been bruised. An immature man finds it difficult to forgive and forget when his pride is hurt.

Like a child, he keeps score and lashes out, activating

any number of ego defenses because he thinks the world and the people in it are out to get him.

When he becomes a man, he leaves childish ways behind. He stops comparing himself to others and competing with those around him. He is no longer easily angered, keeps no record of wrongs, refuses to engage in offensive conversation, or gossip about friends and acquaintances.

He forgives and forgets when offended because he understands he isn't the center of the universe and the people around him are not out to get him. This once immature male is a man. He is considerate of others and displays a selfless attitude. His peers view him as a success. He must be successful if he can afford to place others before himself—or so his immature friends think.

A mature man exudes trust and confidence in his spouse or loved one. He protects and preserves his marriage and relationships. He's sure that his wife and those who love him will remain faithful even in the aftermath of a silly argument or an unfortunate incident. Hope is the glue that bonds his marriage and relationships together.

Last but not least—a mature man no longer makes reckless assumptions or derives a false sense of superiority from childish beliefs. He's humble, not conceited. He no longer feels the need to boast or exhibit false pride. He accepts his strengths and acknowledges his weaknesses. His self-esteem is strong because he's deeply conscious of the fact that he doesn't have all the answers. His priorities are faith, hope and love, and the greatest of these is love.

Secret Nine
CHARITY BEGINS AT HOME

The word "charity" has—at least in recent times—taken on a narrow meaning. These days, when the term "charity" is used, it often refers to a humanitarian act or the establishment of a benevolent fund for some person or underprivileged segment of society. Charities typically appeal to our compassion for service and contributions for the impoverished or disadvantaged.

Our present generation does not understand that charity has a much broader application than this popular definition. Charity is also important in the context of marriage and romance. Charity is a term of endearment that connotes more meaning than the word "love."

Charity is the highest expression of affection, higher than *Eros, philos,* and *agape,* words also used to describe varying degrees of love.

Charity conveys compassion. Compassion transmits a feeling that literally draws two people closer together.

Many are reluctant to express compassion where it really counts—at home. It seems as if people are afraid of intimacy. The fear restrains them from showing compassion for the person who would appreciate it the most.

You may be willing to show compassion for a friend or an acquaintance because you are able to measure your expression and time it right to get the maximum benefit with the minimum amount of effort. Then you are off again, having indicated you care, when in reality you are only interested in appearances. However, appearing compassionate and being compassionate are two different things.

A woman whose husband left her after 14 years of marriage, wept as she told me how compassionate he had been with people with whom he had worked over the years in various charities. She failed to see he went out of his way to avoid being compassionate with her. When confronted with this fact, she muttered an obscenity and angrily walked away.

Several weeks later, I bumped into her in the supermarket. Her feelings had changed. She realized now that although her ex-husband *acted* compassionate with those who were less fortunate, he wasn't truly compassionate with them either.

One by one, his friends privately told her how he would often make fun of those who were in need. He had confided to them that he was only working at the charity to impress his boss.

The moral of the story is that compassion is a feeling one expresses, not a demonstration that impresses.

True, heartfelt compassion invites intimacy and makes you positively irresistible. Compassion is an intregal part of charity and charity always begins at home.

Service represents another important attribute of charity. Few can resist the person who willingly lends a hand to accomplish some goal or task.

Paradoxically, some people find it easier to render service to others rather than to their spouse or loved one.

Joan shared with me how her ex-husband, Al, spent much of his time helping friends and neighbors complete projects around their houses and never lifted a hand to help her at home.

I knew Al personally. He was a genuinely nice guy, but he enjoyed being with his buddies more than his wife. They always had a cold beer waiting, music blaring and a planned activity after the work was completed. Al reasoned that as long as he used the excuse that he was helping a friend or neighbor, his wife wouldn't mind if he was gone.

He was wrong. His absence made her angry—angry enough so she began having an affair. In time, she left Al and filed for divorce.

Al never behaved as the responsible husband his wife wanted him to be. Moreover, although his "friends" were delighted to have his help, they were only using him. Al was giving help where it was unappreciated, while his wife needed him at home.

Service at home will produce feelings of respect and love. Acts of service have a life of their own. They mysteriously live on in the mind of the beneficiary and reproduce themselves as fond memories and warm thoughts. Best of all, helping your spouse inspires reciprocation in ways that are positively seductive.

Don't miss out on the rewards that come from serving at home. They far outweigh the rewards of serving others.

Contribution represents the third important idea found in the concept of charity. A contribution means more than giving tangible gifts such as money or things. It's a long term contract.

The marriage ceremony is similar to a legal transaction. Vows are exchanged, promises made, and the agreement is witnessed by a host of family and friends. Like any legally binding contract, the language is specific about what each party to the transaction can expect from the other. Good contracts also contain a "catch all" clause. The idea of contribution as an integral part of charity embodies such a provision.

If one party in a relationship is having difficulty deciding whether charity is warranted in a given situation, he or she needs to think in terms of contribution. Anytime an opportunity arises to make a contribution at home you should do so. A contribution can be made in any number of ways.

A contribution takes place whenever you support your spouse in being, doing, and having all they desire. Contribution is an important part of charity because it literally bonds two people together in a common cause or an agreed upon strategy aimed at benefiting one party to the relationship directly, while benefiting the other indirectly.

The direct benefit manifests itself as some accomplishment or achievement. The indirect benefit accrues to the benefactor as goodwill, appreciation and a debt of gratitude that the direct beneficiary is obliged to repay at the appropriate time.

More importantly, the idea of contribution acts as a good faith clause in the marital agreement by guaranteeing a successful relationship no matter what the situation or circumstance. A contribution made at the most opportune time is the capstone to the lovely concept of charity.

Charity as presented here is the ninth secret of love and marriage. In reality, it is number one in love's hierarchy of importance. Every successful relationship or marriage embraces this beautiful concept. Try it at home and see for yourself. The benefits will amaze you.

Secret Ten
LOVE IS ALL THAT REALLY MATTERS

This secret is for men who spend an inordinate amount of time trying to get something, be it a promotion, a better job, a larger house, a nicer car, or more education. It's as if this big competition is taking place and you are feverishly struggling to get all you can before the goodies run out and the game stops.

To compete more effectively in the game of life, most people develop expertise or a niche, which they hope will give them an advantage over the competition.

With this expertise or niche, you take your place in the work force where you define yourself by what you do and what you achieve. If you ask a man to describe himself, he will respond with, "I'm an economist," "I'm a doctor," "I'm a carpenter," or "I'm a teacher."

As the game of life progresses, there are those who seem to chase impossible dreams, striving to achieve still more, yet never finding happiness no matter how much success they attain.

In some ways, a man's lot in life is similar to the mouse who finds himself running faster and faster on an ever spinning wheel, frantically trying to reach an end that doesn't exist. Why is that?

Perhaps the answer is that men think the next accomplishment is the one that will make them happy forever. I know how the thought process goes. I, too, have pursued one thing then another, thinking that happiness was waiting round the corner where a new objective lay just out of reach. However, something always seemed to be missing.

In retrospect, it turns out I was pursuing something more. I was seeking love, the kind of love most men pursue but seldom finds.

Men agonize over first one thing, then another because achievements are important to their self-esteem. Men think the ability to claim first prize is proof positive they are shrewd and capable providers. Above all else, a man wants the woman in his life to think of him as wise and hold him in high esteem for his foresight and ability.

If a man finds success but has no one in his life to appreciate it, he feels like a failure. To a man's way of thinking, taking first place is little cause for celebration if he has no one in his life who'll admire the trophy. This is why millions of men strive so hard to achieve so much, yet feel disappointed although they reach their most cherished goals.

The problem can be easily understood. Women often are not aware that men feel loved and appreciated when they are held in high esteem. On the other hand, men aren't aware women feel loved when their husbands are participating in their lives.

I know first hand that men have trouble with this principle. My wife, for example, really does not care very much about my so-called accomplishments. She's more concerned about whether or not I'm home in time to take part in the evening meal and spend quality time with her and the kids. To her, love is all that really matters.

I know success is important to women, too, but there is an irony here—love is all that really matters to a man. St. Paul first revealed this secret two thousand years ago when he wrote, *"If I speak in the tongues of men and of angels, but have not love, I am only a resounding gong or clanging cymbal. And if I have the gift of prophecy and can fathom all mysteries and all knowledge, and if I have a faith that can move mountains, but have not love, I am nothing. If I give all I possess to the poor and surrender my body to the flames, but have not love, I gain nothing. "*

If love was all that really mattered to Paul, arguably the greatest apostle of all, then love is all that matters to any man who dares to accomplish something great. Invite your wife to read this secret with you if you are a man who is struggling to reach some goal or realize a dream. Afterwards, she will understand that love is all that really matters to you, too. Then it's up to you to love each other like you need to be loved.

Secret Eleven
LOVE OFFERS SECURITY

Everyone wants security—job security or financial security. Some want to feel secure in their home or in their neighborhood. Others need to feel secure in a relationship or marriage. However, of all the areas where security seems important, marriage stands out as the one place where it is absolutely critical.

The opportunity to meet new people and make new friends occurs often. There is always another job. Jobs mean money and with money you can buy another house. Losing a marriage is altogether different. It is by far the most painful loss one can ever experience. Even losing a loved one to death can't compare to the pain of losing a spouse to divorce. The sting of death will eventually subside after a season of mourning, but the loss of a marriage can have long-term effects on your emotional, mental and physical well-being.

If you have ever lost a spouse to divorce, or been close to someone who has, you know what I mean. The heartache and misery are beyond words. No other form of security may be as integral to your happiness and health as a feeling of security in your marriage.

Does your marriage possess this essential element? Are you secure? Is your spouse secure? If you answered "yes," then you are among the fortunate few who know the peaceful solace that comes from feeling secure in your relationship. If you answered "no," a feeling of insecurity is haunting you and you need help.

Help can be found in one of the most romantic stories told in the Old Testament. As the story goes, God spoke to a beautiful prophet in Israel named Deborah. He said, "Go

46

tell Barak, a bold young Israelite warrior, to take ten thousand men to Mount Tabor where I will give him the army of Jabin."

Jabin was a king of Canaan who had enslaved the Israelites and cruelly oppressed them for some twenty years. In spite of the prevailing circumstances, Deborah did as God commanded She went to Barak and told him what God had said to her.

Barak, realizing the challenge that lay before him, replied, "I will go only if you will go with me, Deborah."

She answered, "I will go with you, Barak."

With Deborah by his side, Barak went on to free Israel from a cruel oppressor.

What made Barak successful? The answer can be summed up in a word—security. Barak, the mighty warrior, felt secure in his relationship with Deborah. He knew that no matter what he faced, she would be there with him.

If a feeling of security made the difference in Barak's military endeavors, it can make the difference in your marriage as well. "I will go with you wherever you go," will be the most encouraging words your spouse will ever hear you say. Maybe those are the words you need to hear as well.

Millions of people have missed this important truth and suffer needlessly from feelings of insecurity. Often, these feelings are interpreted as anxiety attacks, loneliness, chronic depression or unexplained anger, while the real problem goes undetected. When the fear that accompanies this terrifying feeling causes frightened souls to act out in ways that mask the real issue, their relationship is in for serious trouble.

Julian, an acquaintance of mine, seemed terrified of losing his wife, Margaret. He watched her every move. He kept tabs on her phone calls. He would not allow her to go out with her friends. He called her at work at least a dozen times a day. At night, he made sure she went to bed the same time he did.

Margaret began to fear Julian. He seemed angry all of the time and she never knew when he might unleash another tirade of baseless accusations. This went on for many years until Margaret lost touch with her friends and family. Finally, Margaret grew weary of living under Julian's thumb and she left him.

A few months later she filed for divorce and not long afterwards their marriage was over—all because of Julian's feelings of insecurity.

Janice, another acquaintance of mine, also suffered from insecurity. It began when she became suspicious of her husband. He often spoke of a female friend at work with whom he had coffee in the morning. Sometimes he ate lunch with her, too.

To make matters worse, Janice and her husband were seldom physically intimate with each other and she sensed he might be having an affair with his friend.

Soon, Janice was having panic attacks. She would suddenly feel overwhelmed with anxiety while driving in traffic or fear the worst when her children became ill. As time went on, a cold distance grew between Janice and her husband. She became obsessed with washing her hands, checking the household appliances and monitoring her children's whereabouts.

Over time, Janice began experiencing colon problems. She had difficulty eating. As Janice's anxiety increased her health deteriorated to the point where medical attention became necessary. Tests came back with negative results. Her doctor was stumped. At this point, Janice took the advice of a friend and consulted a therapist.

After several counseling sessions, the root cause of Janice's problem surfaced. She was suffering from an acute fear of losing her husband and her anxiety level was playing havoc with her health.

Luckily, Janice's husband agreed to see the therapist with her. Subsequently, he was able to reassure Janice that he loved her and that he was not having an affair. As counseling progressed, their sex life improved.

Today, Janice no longer suffers from anxiety. She and her husband enjoy a wonderful relationship. They feel secure with each other.

Betty has a slightly different story, but it too involves the painful feeling of insecurity. Betty complains that when she looks into the mirror she sees an unattractive, overweight, middle-aged woman staring back at her and she feels depressed.

To sooth her fears, she frequently points out her imaginary faults to her husband, hoping to hear words of encouragement in return. Instead, he refuses to acknowledge her insecurity. Betty continues to nag him with her inadequacies and struggle with depression.

I know the people in our examples very well. Every time, the insecure party experienced some form of abandonment or rejection during childhood. Each expected the terrible experience to revisit them in their present circumstances. In defense, they retreated to an inner world of isolation and loneliness. They tried to numb their fear with compulsive behavior and stayed emotionally absent from their marriage.

Insecure people are often too preoccupied with their insecurity to be in the moment. Because of the dysfunctional way in which they cope with their insecurity, they unwittingly live a self-fulfilling prophecy.

If the insecure spouse could have seen the root cause of their problem, they might have found reassurance in their partner rather than in the arms of another. If the insecure spouse could have only believed they were loveable, a feeling of security might have relieved feelings of depression and loneliness. If the insecure spouse could have experienced a feeling of security, their anxiety might have been avoided.

What can a feeling of security lend to your marriage? Simply stated, security means you belong to each other and you belong together, forever! Stop right where you are and say to your spouse, "I will go with you wherever you go. I will never leave you nor forsake you, no matter what."

With this mighty declaration of love and support, you will have added the vital ingredient known as security to your relationship or marriage. Without delay, do it today. Give each other the precious bond of security. You will be glad you did.

Secret Twelve
LOVE IS AN EMOTION

Like any emotion love can be here today and gone tomorrow. It's the fickle side of love that causes us to vacillate in our feelings for each other.

"How could I have loved him then, and feel nothing for him now?" is a common refrain.

Regrettably, the frequent answer is, "I guess I must not have really loved him, otherwise I would still feel something for him." The marriage or relationship is terminated, leaving the jilted party feeling confused and wondering what happened.

What happened was the direct result of love's temperamental nature. Unfortunately, too many people don't pay attention to its unpredictability.

Have you, or someone you know, been victimized by love without ever understanding why? Are you going through this heart wrenching experience? Are you confused over what it is you're feeling? If this describes you or someone you know, there's good news. An antidote is available for the emotional trials that accompany the feeling of love—it is called a decision. A decision will ensure that love remains, long after the feeling begins to wane.

Jill and Dale were married a little more than twelve years when he told her he wanted a divorce. The news came as a shock. They had just returned from a wonderful vacation together and everything seemed to be going fine. Now Dale wanted out and Jill could not understand why.

Later, as Jill shared the last year of her marriage with me, I began to sense that her husband was wrestling with a decision. His actions and comments made it clear that he

51

was trying to decide whether he loved his wife or not and whether he should stay in the marriage. When I made this observation to Jill, she said Dale told her he felt his love for her had faded and he was experiencing stronger feelings for a woman he was involved with at work.

What Dale felt isn't anything new. Millions of people go through it each day. Love is a feeling. Today, you may feel differently from what you felt yesterday. Still, that doesn't mean the feeling is gone forever. It may be temporarily replaced by another feeling that can't be trusted either. A conscious, rational, thought process is needed. The mind is the chamber where the process takes place, not the heart.

Similarly, when you feel as if you love someone it's critical to explore the feeling to find out whether it's legitimate or based on infatuation. If you fail to do so, you will invite your feelings to play havoc with your life.

The mind is the guardian of our emotions. Without the mind to chaperon the emotions, you would be left at the whimsical mercy of love. A decision is of paramount importance.

The decision is one that you must make. No one can make it for you, although most of us wish someone else could.

Will you decide to love him forever? Or will you decide that he no longer meets your specifications and pursue someone who does? Will you decide to love him even when you don't feel like it? Or will you decide to allow a temporary loss of feeling or an infatuation with someone else lead you into an affair that could destroy your marriage or relationship?

Will you decide to love her unreservedly? Or will you love her only when you feel like it? Will you decide to love her when the excitement is gone? Or will you fall for someone because of the way they make you feel? These are just some of the decisions a person must make.

52

In the case of Jill and Dale, he made a decision that cost him dearly.

Several months after Dale left Jill, his affair with the woman at the office was over and he wanted to come back home. By then Jill had come to the decision she no longer loved Dale.

Understanding the importance of a decision is one thing, considering what it entails is quite another. Clearly, a decision requires thought. Dale gave his feelings lots of thought but the more he thought, the more confused he became. Here is where decision making comes in. It stops an obsessive thought process that can lead us in the wrong direction, thereby invalidating the feeling forever. No matter how much the feeling vacillates, it can come back again if you are careful to make the right decision.

For anyone who has difficulty making decisions, consider the following definition. Making a decision means committing yourself to a specific result, then cutting yourself off from any other possibility. The word decision comes from the Latin roots "*de*," meaning "from," and "*caedere*," meaning "to cut." When you make a decision to love someone in spite of how you feel, you cut yourself off from any other option. That is it. It's done! You no longer consider any other possibility.

A one-time decision, however, will not a marriage make. A decision made once, sometime in the past, will not a marriage keep. Love is a day-by-day commitment requiring numerous decisions. Make a brand new decision about love each day.

A decision has a powerful effect. It vanishes uncertainty and clears a channel for positive action rather than lingering in neglectful passivity. Indecision is a decision not to decide and it can lead to disastrous results.

Make a decision about your feelings and decide wisely. Whether you decide in favor of a new relationship or stay in your current one, the dilemma is still the same.

Love will wane as all emotions do. A one time decision will not suffice. Despite how you feel at any given point in time, it takes a decision to ensure love remains long after the emotion fades.

Don't lose at love because you relied on a feeling. You can choose to protect your love. A decision is all that is required. Without delay, decide today to love each other "till death do you part." Seal your love with a decision before you seal it with a kiss.

Secret Thirteen

Secret Thirteen
LOVE TO LIVE

An abundant life consists of lots of good friends and healthy relationships.

Hopefully, you understand you have to stay on good terms with co-workers if you want to remain productive, compete for promotions and retain your job. Likewise, you are often willing to forgive your friends when they offend you because you understand how valuable they are to your recreational enjoyment.

You may realize the importance of maintaining harmony with friends and co-workers, but somehow miss the importance of harmony when it comes to your spouse. Why is that?

The answer may be you don't think it's necessary. At least, not in the same way you think it is at the office, factory, golf course or bridge table. Consequently, you act as if you have an option when it comes to your spouse. "Maybe I'll forgive her and maybe I won't." It depends on the nature of the wrong, how long it's been since the offense occurred and what degree of penitence he or she has shown.

Calvin held a grudge against his wife when she seemed disinterested in his minor aches and pains. While he nursed his grudge, he would pout by sticking his nose in a book or newspaper and refuse to look at his wife or listen to her complaints. Meanwhile, Calvin dealt with his co-workers and friends on a give and take basis by forgiving them. Things were going great for Calvin professionally and socially, but life at home was another matter.

Calvin would hold a grudge for two or three weeks then, inexplicably, forgive his wife and resume normal communication with her. When she finally asked him why he held a grudge so long, he responded by telling her it took a certain amount of time for him to get over the hurt she had caused him.

What Calvin meant, but didn't say, was it took a certain amount of time for him to feel as if he had punished her enough for her snub.

Tracie used a similar tactic with her husband, Roy. When he spent too much time with his friends and ignored her, she would spend several days shopping with friends and ignore him. Then she would forgive him because she felt that she had gotten even.

Some spouses don't forgive as quickly as Tracie and Calvin. They hold a grudge against their wife or husband for months and sometimes years for wrongs real or imagined. In the process they make themselves and their spouses miserable without ever stopping to think about the detrimental effects their actions are having on their marriage and on them.

Disharmony in marriage will only produce discontentment and dissatisfaction. Any benefits you may derive from your relationships with co-workers and friends will never make up for disharmony at home.

Your spouse is the most important person in your life. If he or she wasn't, his or her actions would never bother you. You would feel indifferent whenever he or she did or said something that seemed troublesome.

Here is the secret to understanding just how important your spouse is to you. Friends and co-workers only know as much about you as you are willing to reveal, thus their offenses are only relevant in a professional or social context. You tend to forgive them more quickly than you do your spouse.

Your spouse knows you inside and out. No one knows you better so actions take on added meaning. If you are not careful, you may interpret a misspoken word or errant act as criticism, rejection or potential abandonment of you.

The difference should tell you that your relationship with your spouse is more important than any other. Sadly, for some it's not a question of whether to admit it or not, they are simply unaware of this powerful truth.

Recognize and accept the role your spouse plays in your life. It takes harmony at home to live life to the fullest. Underestimating your relationship with your spouse will leave you feeling partially complete.

Drop any grudge you are holding against your spouse. When you do, you will experience the joy and contentment that come from living life to the fullest. You may be well aware of the many reasons why you should forgive your co-workers and friends. Why not forgive your spouse too?

Love to live. Forget and forgive. If you do, you will solve all of your relationship problems and live life the way it was meant to be lived—abundantly.

Secret Fourteen
LOVE IS SELFLESS

Genuine love asks only that you think of yourself less, not less of yourself. Constantly dwelling on your short-comings robs you of the time and ability to think of your spouse or loved one because you are too absorbed in yourself to think of anyone else.

Ironically, dwelling on what you think is wrong with you won't change anything. It only compounds feelings of inferiority. By dwelling on your deficiencies, real or imagined, in effect you are pointing out to those around you just how insecure and self-centered you really are. Thinking of yourself less is more conducive to building healthy relationships than thinking less of yourself.

Thinking of yourself less allows you to forget yourself and experience the kind of joy and contentment in life that can only be felt when your attention is directed at someone else. When you become obsessed with yourself, you lose.

The ability to forget oneself by focusing on the other person is the distinguishing trait of all enduring relation-ships. Take Laura and Max for example.

This fortunate couple had just finished celebrating their 25th wedding anniversary when I first met them. They impressed me, not only with the number of years they had been married, but by the way they cared about each other.

What made their marriage special? When I asked Laura, she replied, "Ours is a selfless love." She added that neither she nor Max makes a practice of complaining about their individual problems, personal needs or private ailments. Instead, they took it upon themselves to show concern for each other while forgetting themselves.

Those close to this lucky couple tell me what Laura and Max shared with me is really true. After observing their marriage first hand, I came away wanting what they had.

Unfortunately, many couples are so absorbed in themselves they have little time for their spouse or anyone else. Rick and Linda are an illustration. Rick and Linda habitually whined about their puny ailments, minor inconveniences and trivial faults. Each wanted the other's sympathy. Rick wanted Linda to understand what he was going through at work and Linda wanted the same from Rick. Each of them was into themselves and intent on pointing out their problems to each other. They focused their attention on everything wrong in their lives and failed to see the good in their marriages.

When their marriage ended, Rick seemed shocked and surprised. I was surprised he noticed it was over. They were both so immersed in their petty problems that neither had time for the other.

Any line of thinking has extremes, such as the difficulties caused by thinking less of yourself than you should. If you think you are inadequate, flawed or less than those around you, you are suffering from a deep-seated inferiority complex that will produce disrespect, dependency and infidelity in your relationship or marriage. Carol is a case in point.

After talking with Carol, it became clear she struggled with feelings of inadequacy and guilt. She seemed convinced she didn't deserve the good things in life. As with most people who suffer from feelings of inferiority, the facts didn't support the image others had of her.

Carol was pretty, smart and personable. Her career was going well, her superiors liked her and she was the most popular person in her office.

Carol's feelings of inferiority played a major role in her decision to marry Bob. Although he seemed to have problems of his own, Carol felt she could not afford to let him get away. An opportunity like this might never come again.

A review of Bob and Carol's marriage is revealing. Carol's husband also felt unworthy. His track record showed he rejected anyone who was genuinely interested in him. Bob felt something had to be wrong with someone who would stoop so low as to befriend him.

True to form, Bob grew to disrespect Carol. He eventually left her for another woman—a woman who refused to treat him as well as Carol had.

Could Carol's problems have been avoided? Absolutely. If she had thought more of herself, she might have married a man who possessed a healthy self-esteem of his own. Instead, her self doubt, fear of rejection and low self-esteem produced a dysfunctional relationship that had no chance at succeeding.

The secret here is that you possess gifts and talents uniquely yours. Furthermore, you have an inheritance and a purpose all your own. To think otherwise is to imagine you lack something others have. This delusion always results in self-centered behavior.

Appreciate yourself. Love yourself. Bask in the truth of whom you are. To know the truth is to discover freedom from inferiority, fear and self-doubt. Better yet, this marvelous truth will liberate you from the tendency to think less of yourself and enable you to think of yourself less.

All successful marriages are composed of two people who appreciate themselves and know their true worth. They can invest their time and curiosity in their spouse or loved one, and in return, receive the love and attention they want and deserve.

Remember. You are special! Special enough that you can afford to think of yourself less. Don't, under any circumstances, think less of yourself than you should. A

wonderful relationship awaits you if you follow this simple
advice.

Secret Fifteen
BUILD YOUR LOVE ON SOLID GROUND

True love is constructed on a firm foundation, not on shifting sand. Real love will endure while a mere facsimile will not.

"What type of foundation is firm enough to build a relationship on?" you ask. The answer can be found in the story of the two builders.

One builder constructed his home on a shifting substance—much like the finely textured sand found along the peaceful Pacific coastline. The second builder constructed his house on firm bedrock—the same granite like surface that anchors lighthouses to the eastern seaboard as they stand watch over the tempestuous Atlantic.

As the story goes, the rains descended, the floods came, the winds blew and the one who built his house on sand watched as it collapsed under the tumultuous storm. "And great was the fall of it," is the story's chilling refrain.

Meanwhile, the person who built his house on rock experienced the same storms as the house constructed on the foundation made of sand. The storms smashed against the house with the fury that destroyed the first builder's home, but the house standing on a firm foundation would not fall.

The story doesn't stop there, however. It goes on to identify the two builders. The first builder is called foolish. He built his house on sand. The second builder is revered for his foresight and wisdom. He was wise. He built his house on a firm foundation.

You may dismiss the story as too simplistic or far too

abstract to be applicable to you. However, the tempest that destroyed the house constructed on sand symbolizes the storms of life that will inevitably blow your way, putting your marriage or relationship to the test.

A closer look at the two builders would be prudent, for the story reveals an interesting point. A relationship built on steadfast principals will withstand the storms of life, while a relationship built on loose values and changing mores will not.

The failure of a relationship or marriage causes tremendous pain. It is never a small thing to lose a home, a family, a relationship or marriage. I discovered firsthand how painful it is to lose a marriage and a home. I know others who have lost marriages and homes. I also know those who have lost precious relationships with children and friends. They will tell you the price for building on shifting sand is high.

How fortunate are those who build on a firm foundation and anchor their marriage or relationship to a bedrock of solid principles. The construction of their relationship or marriage appears truly grand. The walls are strong and footings are set in unshakable soil. The architecture will withstand inclement weather and changing seasons. The roof provides an impregnable defense against wind, rain and hail. When the storms of life assail, their relationship or marriage will not fail, for it is built on firm bedrock.

What characterizes an immoveable foundation? Although there are several important properties, honesty heads the list. A discerning friend once told me, "Honesty will always lead you in the direction you need to go." The probability of your marriage or relationship succeeding, increases significantly when it is founded on honesty.

Honesty means telling the truth. Several situations can frustrate you in this area, and they are just as difficult for women as they are for men. One involves telling your spouse where you have been. This frequently happened to me after an evening of drinking, gambling or being unfaithful. My advice here is simple. Don't go places where you would be ashamed to be seen and don't pursue experiences that produce feelings of guilt.

Another situation involves the infamous "spending spree." Some women find it difficult to explain their spending habits, especially if they spend money foolishly or lavishly. Explaining how you manage your money, including where you spend it and how much you spend, can prove difficult for anyone. Dishonesty over matters involving money is one of the most destructive storms any relationship can experience. If you can't trust each other with money, chances are your marriage is built on shifting sand.

Trust is also necessary for a firm foundation. Trust is a belief in each other that transcends any unfortunate circumstance life may blow your way. Trusting your spouse means giving him or her the benefit of the doubt, not second guessing them by questioning their loyalty or motives. Mistrusting each other never results in anything good. In fact, it often inspires the distrusted spouse to engage in mischief.

Trust instills a feeling of responsibility in the person on whom you have bestowed your faith and confidence. It stimulates within them the desire to feel trustworthy. Trusting each other is the preferred option. Couples who mistrust each other, and constantly demonstrate their mistrust with suspicion, skepticism and paranoia are building on sinking sand.

Unselfishness is the third characteristic found in any firm foundation. Thinking about what you can give rather than what you can get is the strongest material anyone can use to build a lasting marriage or relationship. Experience tells me men contend with the problem of selfishness more

64

than women.

Women, quite naturally, act out of a maternal instinct. This is not necessarily good, particularly if it enables their husband to continue to live selfishly.

In both men and women, selfishness embodies an "I want what I want when I want it" attitude. No one else matters. The only thing that counts is *me*. Even in moments of kindness, self-centered individuals may hide bad motives under good ones. Selfishness is the porous texture that constitutes sinking sand.

Purity is the fourth component found in a solid foundation. Purity means virtue, decency, morality and innocence.

Couples who fail to pursue a virtuous, decent and moral lifestyle fall prey to the temptations that periodically come their way. Temptations are some of the fiercest storms you will ever face. Any marriage or relationship that lacks virtues and morals is standing on shaky ground.

The final building block found in any successful relationship or marriage is love.

Everyone experiences a multitude of emotions in life—passion, desire and sensuality are a few. Even fear, worry, envy and anxiety are sensations that are part of each person's natural range of emotions, yet none of them are comparable to love.

I married the first time because all my friends were getting married and I was afraid I would never find anyone else who would want to marry me.

I married the second time for different reasons. I was lonely and afraid, and I wanted someone to take care of me—someone who would never leave me.

It may sound preposterous, but millions of people marry for similar reasons. They frequently enroll in the divorce recovery groups I lead. Like myself and many others, they built their marriage on a shifting foundation.

Have you built your relationship or marriage on firm

bedrock? Is it constructed on honesty, trust, unselfishness, purity and, above all, love? You will know when the storms of life blow your way.

"But what if some of these pieces are missing in my marriage or relationship? Is there still hope?" you are wondering.

The answer is a resounding "yes!" Start today to fill the cracks in your foundation with the missing pieces so it will support your marriage through all life's storms.

Secret Sixteen
THE MIRACLE OF CANA

Having failed at marriage twice, I wanted desperately to find the secret to a lasting relationship. I read self-help books, visited counselors and talked to well-meaning friends until I was exhausted with my efforts. Then, one day I read about a wedding that took place at Cana in Galilee two thousand years ago. I found the secret I'd been searching for.

What secret did I discover? To answer the question, consider several factors.

First, Jesus was there. He could have been anywhere else that day but He chose to attend the wedding at Cana. Remember, He was here in human form and could only be in one place at a time. The choice about where to spend His day was extremely important. His presence at the wedding in Cana is significant because of the distance He had to travel to get there from Nazareth, the city where He lived.

Third, a miracle took place during the wedding celebration. Not an ordinary miracle, but one of renowned importance because it was the first miracle performed by Jesus. A miracle in which He turned water into wine.

I must admit, I wondered why Jesus would turn water into wine for a wedding party at Cana when He could have chosen a more serious problem on which to work a miracle. Also, why did the disciple report the miracle at Cana in his Gospel and keep the newlyweds' identities a secret? Since Jesus thought enough of this lucky couple to attend their wedding and use the occasion to perform His first miracle, why don't we know more about them?

Ask any theologian the same set of questions and they will tell you Jesus chose to attend the wedding at Cana because He knew he would find a large crowd of people there. The theory being He wanted to work His first miracle in front of a large audience and thereby proclaim His earthly mission and divine nature for all the world to see. Stated another way, Jesus cared little about the couple or their wedding. He only used the occasion to promote his reputation and advance his own agenda.

I believe the theologians are wrong because their answers fail to explain why Jesus would choose the wedding at Cana rather than a more serious problem closer to Nazareth to demonstrate His Divine nature. Neither does it explain the heart of Jesus. He always put others first. He cared for people too much to use them to promote his own interests or to advance His reputation.

If you recall the life and times of Jesus, you'll remember He usually tried to avoid crowds. He was even reluctant to perform the miracle at Cana, but He did so at His mother's insistence. To put it bluntly, Jesus wasn't a show-off. That was not His style.

Better answers to our questions than the theologians have to offer are available. I believe Jesus's presence at the wedding of Cana illustrates how important marriage is in the eyes of God. In fact, I believe marriage is Heaven's highest priority.

I also believe I know why the disciple of Jesus left the identity of the couple at Cana out of his Gospel. I have an idea he hoped you would write your name in the story, and you would experience the miracle of Cana for yourself.

For the miracle, Jesus turned ordinary water into superb wine. Notice that He didn't add water to the residue of wine left over in the wineskins and shake it about. This would have produced cheap wine, wine far too inferior for those united in holy matrimony.

However, the miracle at Cana is not about turning water into wine. It's more. The miracle symbolizes a transformation that takes place when a man and woman are changed by the power of love from the persons they used to be to brand new persons.

This astounding miracle can be experienced in any marriage or relationship. You may be experiencing it yourself. Or maybe you have watched it take place in someone else's life.

If you haven't experienced the miracle firsthand, take heart. The good news is you can experience it, too. The word "gospel" means "good news." The disciple who recorded the miracle at Cana included it in his Gospel because he wanted you to know the couple at Cana can be you. You, too, can change from the persons you used to be to someone altogether new by the power of love.

This wonderful miracle has occurred in marriages all over the world. It happened in mine. The good news is that I know it can happen in your marriage or relationship, too.

Here is a small taste of my personal miracle. My wife and I are different in many ways. We come from different socioeconomic backgrounds. She is twelve years younger than I am. She has not had a problem with alcohol or other addictions. She has never been divorced.

In spite of all of our apparent differences, we're living proof that the Miracle of Cana can still take place in the hearts and lives of two who will allow their love for each other to transform them into a happy and contented couple.

If you are interested in this miracle, I have a simple formula that will help you experience it for yourself. First, identify the areas in your lives where you differ. Next, tell each other you won't allow your differences to come between you. Then accept each other and love each other unconditionally. When you do, you will be transformed from who you are to someone better. Love will change you as surely as water was changed into wine.

Part Two

The Painful Problems
of Love & Marriage

Secret Seventeen
CAUSES AND SOLUTIONS

This section begins the discussion of the primary causes of love's painful problems, causes that surfaced time and again in divorce recovery groups with which I have been associated over the years.

Approximately sixty percent of the participants in my groups experienced difficulties in their marriages because either they or their estranged spouse grew up with an alcoholic parent. These ill-fated individuals became passive doormats who avoided trouble at any cost by acting their way through adolescence.

If it wasn't their theatrical prowess that got them by, it was their uncanny ability to blend into the woodwork or to simply disappear at the appropriate time, thereby escaping the alcoholic's wrath.

Others who grew up in alcoholic homes learned to place the needs of a self-centered, or unreasonably demanding parent before their own. Almost without exception, they married an alcoholic or someone with alcoholic tendencies.

The workaholic is the second major cause of marital problems for those who have participated in my divorce recovery groups. Workaholics immerse themselves in their careers and derive their self-esteem from their accomplishments. The problems introduced into the family system by the workaholic spouse are every bit as damaging as those caused by the alcoholic. Like the alcoholic, the workaholic is always missing at the most crucial times. They seem terrified of intimacy and unable to express their feelings. He or she secretly believes that getting too close might expose their inadequacies as a person and a spouse.

My experience indicates that painful childhood memories represent the third major cause of divorce. If either the husband or wife experienced some form of emotional or physical abandonment as an adolescent, the memory seems to stifle their ability to achieve intimacy in their marriage and other adult relationships.

Disclosures are becoming more commonplace as the victims of abuse defy feelings of guilt and shame to seek the healing light of truth and acceptance.

Knowing what is known about the root causes of love's painful problems, it shouldn't surprise you that the people who enroll in the divorce recovery groups I facilitate are asked to examine their childhood. They often discover they married the person who most closely mirrored a shaming authority figure from the past.

Others realize they recreated the environment they grew up in, even to the point of resurrecting the roles they were accustomed to seeing themselves or their parents star in at home. Most perpetuated the same destructive behavior, unworkable beliefs and self-defeating attitudes their parents modeled.

Take Jason's experience. His father and grandfather were both alcoholics. Their thinking patterns and inappropriate behavior seemed normal to a child with no one else to look up to. Naturally, Jason took their pessimistic outlook and alcoholic coping strategies into adulthood where he proceeded to ruin two marriages.

When Jason entered a divorce recovery program, he knew nothing about alcoholism or its devastating effects. Today Jason understands how his childhood negatively impacted his life.

Patricia also grew up in a dysfunctional home. Her father was the CEO of a large financial institution, He chose to spend 70 hours a week at work.

When Patricia was cast in the lead role in the eighth grade musical, her father was closing a deal on a large shopping center. A year later when she sang in the freshman glee club, he was out of town on business. When she received a scholastic honor for her work on the school newspaper, he was entertaining a group of foreign bankers at a local restaurant.

After Patricia graduated from college she met and married a man just like her father—emotionally unavailable. Her marriage ultimately ended in divorce.

Patricia eventually found her way into a divorce recovery group where she learned how her relationship with her father prepared her for more heartache later in life. Today, Patricia realizes she is worthy of a man who is capable of giving her the love and support she deserves.

Philip also experienced abandonment as a child. His mother left him and his father shortly before his eighth birthday. He all but raised himself. The experience left Philip bitter and angry toward women in general.

As an adult, Philip tried and failed at several marriages. His deep-seated anger seemed to have a way of rearing its ugly head at the most inopportune time.

Finally, Philip sought help and was directed to a divorce recovery group. He came to realize how his earlier experience with abandonment had affected his marriages. He decided to face his unresolved issues and forgive his mother.

Philip is in another relationship and he is happier than he has ever been. All because he examined his past and confronted the root cause of his relational and marital problems.

What does all this have to do with causes and solutions? It would have been easy for Jason, Patricia and Philip to wind up in another unhealthy marriage. Lots of people seem to bounce from one unhealthy relationship to the other without ever understanding why.

Thank God for divorce recovery groups and those who find answers in their nonjudgmental program of recovery.

They are wise enough to realize something is not only wrong with their ex-spouse, but with themselves as well. They courageously seek solutions to their problems and go on to build meaningful relationships and successful marriages with someone else.

What about you? Have you faced your personal demons? Do you see why you think and act the way you do? It's important to explore your personal history and identify the reasons for your actions. Understanding why you made the mistakes you made helps to put the past in perspective and enable you to do better in the future. Facing the past allows us to move ahead, while refusing to do so will only keep us stuck.

Don't fear the past. Don't shrink from the pain. Don't repress the memories. Get them out. Confront them. Grieve about them. Then take responsibility for where you are now, and for what you are presently experiencing in your relationship or marriage.

You are not responsible for your childhood or the people and events that made it what it was, but you are responsible now. You have the power to change. The secret to your power is in your pain. When you are sick and tired of living the way you do, you will look at your past and change what needs to be changed in you.

Those who have participated in support groups have felt something truly remarkable happen. Their lives have been radically changed for the better and their secret can be your secret too.

Secret Eighteen
LOVE AND SEX

Love and sex are the two most sought after experiences in the entire world. In their haste to discover both, many have mistaken sex for love. Others have underestimated the importance of sex, wanting to experience love instead. You may experience sex without feeling loved. Conversely, you may feel loved without having sex. Ask any couple and I'm sure they would agree putting both together in a meaningful relationship can be difficult. For example, I'll begin with Mark and Sherry.

Mark was twenty years old when he married Sherry. She had just turned nineteen. From the beginning, Mark wanted to achieve sexual intimacy with his young bride but she would reject his advances saying she had a headache and didn't feel well. Mark loved his wife and hoped her headaches would eventually go away. However, they persisted.

As the months passed, Mark argued frequently with Sherry over their lack of physical intimacy. Sherry always seemed to win the battle but Mark was secretly planning to win the war. Mark decided that since his wife refused to have sex with him he would go elsewhere to get his needs met. He began visiting massage parlors and porno shops. He even thought seriously about having an affair. All the while Sherry refused to give herself to Mark and her headaches continued.

Unbeknownst to Mark, Sherry wanted emotional intimacy most of all. However, Mark was afraid of intimacy, preferring sex instead.

Mark wasn't entirely to blame for his fear. His parents taught him men should always be "strong." Emotions were irrational expressions of weak-minded individuals. No one hugged or touched each other at the house in which Mark grew up. Close physical contact was taboo. Mark learned to repress his feelings and avoid any physical contact involving touching or hugging. Touchy, feely stuff was for sissies but getting close to someone was okay if the purpose was to have sex.

Sherry's background was quite different from Mark's. Her strict religious upbringing taught that sex was sinful. To make matters worse, Sherry's older sister had gotten pregnant when she was a high school freshmen. Her parents shamed her to the point that she had to leave home. The experience left Sherry with sexual hangups impossible to work through on her own.

Mark and Sherry fought over sex for several years. Finally Mark had an affair and Sherry found out. She was devastated and filed for divorce. A few months later their marriage was over, all because they neglected to search for the root cause of their problem.

Next, consider the relationship of Vince and Kathy.

On a hot summer evening Vince met Kathy at a swank nightclub on the fashionable side of town. From the moment they laid eyes on each other, it was magic. The music and the moment produced an intoxicating spell as they danced the night away. When the music stopped the morning sun found them wrapped in each others arms, spent from a torrid night of sex.

No one could blame Vince and Kathy for the attraction they felt for each other. Kathy was beautiful—stunning actually. Vince was a handsome, athletically built young man. He was intelligent, too.

As one might expect, their relationship intensified over the next several months. Sex was great and getting better. Then, with all the flare of a modern day Valentino, Vince asked Kathy to marry him. She accepted.

Their whirlwind affair felt like a fairy tale as they

pledged their love at the altar of matrimony a few months later.

Six months into their marriage, Kathy fell in love with another man and she filed for divorce.

Vince was in a state of shock as he relayed the details of his storybook romance to his divorce recovery group. Weeping, he confessed that infatuation had gotten the best of him.

Vince succumbed to lust thinking it was love. His marriage was over in less than a year. Lust, masquerading as love, claimed his heart while another man claimed Kathy. For Vince and Kathy, love was never a part of the equation.

Your problem is different, you say? Then maybe you can relate to Ron.

Ron told his support group that sex between him and his wife was a disaster long before their divorce. Ron revealed they had sex together out of a sense of duty rather than because of their mutual feelings of love and respect for each together.

Ron further revealed he felt guilty after having sex with his wife. He eventually stopped having any physical contact with her, preferring instead to satisfy his sexual urges with pornography and phone sex.

After several weeks in a divorce recovery program Ron admitted that he married his wife because his friends were getting married and he used porn as a way to avoid intimacy with his wife.

Ron's marriage lacked love and eventually it lacked sex too, all because he chose to ignore the importance of both in his marriage.

These examples don't describe your problem either, you are thinking. Maybe Randy's problems with love and sex will be more to the point.

During his marriage to Tina, Randy would sometimes allow his ego to interfere with his sex life. His ego would interject the absurd idea that his marriage was lacking something. "Why else would Tina refuse to comply with my sexual advances?" he wondered. "If she loved me, she would show me by acquiescing to my sexual desires," Randy reasoned.

The problem was that Randy's requests were often too unconventional for Tina. Her conservative attitude toward sex simply would not allow her to indulge in any form of sexual activity that was out of the ordinary. Randy's ego would whisper, "See, I told you she doesn't love you." Then, Randy would sneak off to the massage parlors and strip joints on the seedy side of town to get his needs met.

Luckily, Randy and Tina were interested enough in preserving their marriage to seek professional help. A trained counselor discovered the dynamics of their problem. The real problem, as Randy discovered, was the "trap" set by his ego. Randy grew up in a negative environment so he felt undeserving and unlovable. When his wife refused to satisfy him sexually, his ego would tell him she didn't love him. This rationalization gave him permission to "act out" by taking secret excursions to massage parlors and strip joints on the other side of town.

Randy not only rationalized his adulterous behavior, he also negatively reinforced his belief that he was unlovable. Once Randy understood the trap set by his ego he could design a strategy to counter his destructive behavior and experience emotional and physical intimacy with his wife.

None of these examples describe your marriage, you say. Maybe you and your husband still have strong feelings for each other, but he's had affairs and that confuses you. You decided you can't trust him so you punish him by withholding sex.

With the passage of time, you begin to question your marriage. "What is going on? Is it you? Is it he? Why does he seem to love you, even want you, yet find it difficult to stay away from other women?" you ask.

The answers are really quite simple. Your husband secretly believes if you knew him, you would not like him. When he is having an affair, he feels unconditionally loved. The person with whom he is having an affair knows he is having an affair and "loves" him anyway. He feels he can be himself with her—faults, fantasies and all.

Unfortunately, he is afraid he can't be himself around you due to his low self-esteem. You might see him for whom he really is and stop loving him. If you knew he was capable of having an affair, would you love him? This is only one issue he thinks he must not tell you about. There are others. He thinks if you know what they are, you might like him even less. For you, love is the missing ingredient.

On to William and Penny. They have been married 15 years but their sex life is not rewarding. Penny secretly harbors resentments against William. She keeps a score and wouldn't dare allow herself to become physically intimate with him.

William is keeping a score, too. He can recall each and every time his wife rebuffed his sexual advances. William handles his resentments differently from his wife—he pretends he doesn't care. He has a lady friend at work with whom he is emotionally involved. He satisfies his sexual urges by fantasizing about her.

Neither William nor Penny is happy. They are too in love with their resentments to constructively deal with the issue of sex. Love is definitely missing.

Our final example couple is Robert and Joan. Although Joan was stricken with an illness some years ago that threatened to restrict her sexual activity, Robert continues to love her.

Over the years, Robert and Joan have worked doubly hard at maintaining their relationship. Instead of bemoaning their misfortune, they decided to look at their problem as a chance to make a new start. They slowed they became best friends. As friends, they trust each other enough to please each other sexually in ways they never dreamed of before Joan's illness.

Today, Robert claims his sex life is better than ever and his marriage to Joan has blossomed into an exciting love affair.

Often, men aren't as bold as Robert. They are reluctant to face their sexual problems because they are afraid of intimacy and terrified of feelings.

Too many women aren't like Joan. They are averse to communicating their wants and needs to their husbands believing they will experience rejection if they do. The result is, neither spouse really knows what the other one wants. Each mistakenly assumes they are not loved or that no one cares about them.

When one spouse thinks they are not loved or what they want from the other isn't important, trouble soon follows.

What do you want from your spouse? Is it sex? Is it love? Are you afraid to get close to your spouse and to your feelings? Are you letting negative childhood experiences rob you of the closeness everyone longs for?

Perhaps you are allowing someone else's ideas about sex to influence your sex life. Maybe you and your spouse are both keeping a score? Are you trying to avoid the real problem by escaping to an addiction?

Isn't it time you deal with your problem? Possibly it isn't a compulsive behavior preventing you from experiencing emotional and physical intimacy. Conceivably, you simply need to talk to each other and allow each other to know the truth about you, your past, your childhood and your beliefs.

Think about reevaluating your idea of love and sex. Have you mistaken lust for love, intensity for intimacy and control for caring? Exorcize those nagging resentments and allow your spouse back into your life.

Whatever the issue is, talk about it. Start talking and don't stop. There is no better way to start a friendship. It might even lead to a satisfying sex life.

Work on your relationship. Like Robert and Joan, you may become friends as well as lovers.

Secret Nineteen
BLIND LOVE

Don't confuse the expression "love is blind" with the term "blind love." Cindy did and her heart was broken.

Cindy grew up in an environment void of emotional support. Her parents were too busy to give her the attention she needed. Although Cindy excelled in school, she was not especially popular with her classmates. She seldom dated as a teenager. Things changed, however, when Cindy went off to college. She was suddenly a lovely young lady with grace and charm. All the boys wanted to date her but her self-esteem remained undernourished and in need of repair.

During the first few months at school, Cindy was introduced to a young man named Eli. She immediately fell for him. No one could blame Cindy. Eli appeared to have it all and he talked of impressive things to come. Nevertheless, as the school year wore on, he began to drop classes. At the close of the second semester, he had completed only six hours of course work.

The next year wasn't any different. Eli enrolled in one course after the other, only to drop out with an incomplete grade half way through the semester. He found employment at several businesses near campus, only to quit after a few days on the job. Eli could not seem to finish anything he started. In spite of Eli's problems, Cindy continued to believe in him. Although Cindy could have any guy she wanted, she felt hopelessly in love with Eli.

As time passed, Eli asked Cindy to help him with his course work. Cindy thought maybe she could help Eli stay in school. She agreed. Her attempts to help continued until Eli lost interest in his studies altogether and dropped out of

Eli lost interest in his studies altogether and dropped out of school.

Cindy continued to stick by Eli, giving him emotional support and lending him money when he needed it.

When Eli's parents discovered he was no longer taking classes, their financial support stopped and Cindy became his primary source for money. Somehow Cindy managed to complete her undergraduate work and enroll in a master's program.

Meanwhile, Eli developed another problem. He began abusing prescription drugs. His drug use appeared legitimate at first. He said they were prescribed by a doctor to combat a growing problem with depression.

Cindy graduated from college and accepted a job at a local consulting firm. At this time, Eli asked her to marry him. Although Cindy's instincts sounded a warning, she still thought she could help Eli. She agreed to marry him.

Although Eli's dependency on prescription drugs increased in the months preceding their wedding, Cindy reasoned that the doctors knew what they were doing. She married Eli in a little chapel on the outskirts of Las Vegas.

Unfortunately, marriage didn't help. Eli's drug problem worsened, even though Cindy tried to curtail his use of prescriptions.

Two years later, Eli was not only still using drugs, but he was having affairs with other women. Women much younger than Cindy; women who weren't trying to change him; women who used drugs with him.

Cindy was devastated when she found out about the affairs. She thought it was her fault. Maybe she could make it up to Eli by giving him more attention. She told herself that if she changed her hairstyle, bought a new dress, lost weight and accepted his drug use he would find her attractive again. She even tried partying with him, trying to gain his approval. Feelings of inferiority, coupled with the fear of loneliness, obstructed Cindy's judgement.

for several more years. During this period they had a child. Cindy hoped the responsibilities of fatherhood would change Eli. She was wrong. Numerous promises and pledges were made, then broken. The cycle continued unabated until Eli finally left Cindy for another woman and she filed for divorce.

Cindy was searching for answers as she told her story to her divorce recovery group. The other participants helped Cindy see why her marriage failed.

Each in their own words described it as "blind love." Cindy was blind when it came to Eli. She refused to see his faults and examine his motives. Fear told her, "You can't live without him. The loneliness will kill you. You dare not look."

Pride said, "You can help him. It isn't as bad as it seems. He will grow up with a little coercing. You can change him." Blind love caused Cindy nothing but heartache.

What about the expression, "love is blind?" How is it different from the fatal attraction known as "blind love?" Examine Susan's marriage for the answers.

Susan was a young, bright, articulate, college sophomore when she met Robert. He was the most handsome man in her drama class. Tall, debonair and talented, Robert was sure to become a Broadway actor. He can't miss, Susan thought. All the girls wanted Robert—that was obvious. All the boys envied him—that was obvious, too.

Susan and Robert started dating and in only a few short months they fell in love. After graduation, Robert found work in an off Broadway play. Susan took a position with a large investment firm.

Robert's acting career began to go very well. Opportunities started pouring in. Starring roles, thunderous applause and national acclaim followed. Robert asked Susan to marry him. She accepted and a few months later they married.

Several years went by. Robert's career began to stall. He found himself losing leading roles to younger men. Robert became disenchanted and discouraged. His acting career continued to wane. Soon, even supporting parts became scarce.

Luckily, Susan's career began to accelerate. Promoted to district manager, her income doubled. More promotions followed, along with stock options and bonuses. Susan was ascending the corporate ladder as Robert's star continued to fade.

Susan and Robert watched their careers go in opposite directions over the next several years. The problem really wasn't with Robert. He was simply growing older and finding it difficult to compete with the new breed of actors. He began to put on weight, his hair began to turn gray and that old "spark" was missing.

Susan watched as Robert's career slowly died. Soon they were relying solely on her income. Robert struggled with hurt pride. Depressed, he considered his options. He had no other training or experience to draw on. Though times were tough for Robert, Susan never held a negative thought about him. She continued to offer encouragement and support and she still pictured him as her "leading man."

As time passed, Susan realized something had to be done. She challenged Robert to discover the hidden opportunities present in any unfortunate situation. Susan recognized her husband's aptitude for dramatic acting. She knew there had to be a place where he could put his talent to work.

Susan urged Robert to think about all of his experience, his genius for acting, and his love for the theater. She suggested he look for ways to share his talents with others. "Why not teach drama?" she wondered aloud one day. "It would give you an outlet for your talent and a dependable paycheck," she told Robert.

Robert thought about Susan's suggestion. It gave him an idea. Why not approach the local college about teaching a drama class? It might be a way to share my knowledge and experience with other aspiring thespians, he thought.

Robert explored the possibility with officials at a local college. They were interested. Within a year he was placed in charge of a newly formed drama department. Teaching his classes led to the fulfillment that had eluded him since the demise of his acting career.

Several years have gone by and Robert's hair has turned completely gray. He has put on more weight—the years have taken their toll. Nevertheless, Susan still loves him as much as ever.

For Susan, love is blind. She doesn't see an aging actor whose career ended abruptly. She sees a renowned thespian with a wealth of knowledge and experience to offer aspiring performers. To this day, Robert remains her Broadway Star.

I understand the difference between blind love and a love that's blind. Twice I experienced the pain of divorce. I, too, fell victim to blind love.

Today, I can attest that love is blind in many ways. My wife is eleven years younger than I am, yet she sees me as her handsome prince. My hair is graying and it's difficult to keep the weight off, but she doesn't judge me by my looks.

I'm also a recovering alcoholic with an obsessive-compulsive personality. In my wife's eyes, I'm a seeker of serenity and truth. Though I failed at a career in the ministry many years ago, my wife thinks of me as a spiritual person on a journey toward greater enlightenment. For her, love is blind.

Love is blind when you see only the good and accentuate the positive qualities in your spouse and in your relationship. However, I'm not advising anyone to deny the blatant faults and glaring weakness of another. That's blind love and it invites trouble. I strongly encourage anyone who wants to enjoy a healthy relationship to view their loved one with optimism.

Discerning the difference between blind love and love that is blind can be extremely difficult. It is prudent to take the time to assess your marriage or relationship and ask yourself whether your love is blind or whether you are the victim of blind love? There is a big difference. It is up to you to discern the difference. Once you do, you will either find yourself on the road to infinite happiness or in need of recovery and healing.

If you decide you are suffering from blind love, turn it into a tough love. State with conviction and confidence you will not live your life this way any longer—and mean it! Tell your wife or husband exactly what's expected of them and what they can expect of you. Find a support group where others share a similar problem and are moving toward emotional recovery. Look in your phone book, ask your friends, your pastor, a relative or neighbor. One or more of them can tell you where to find a group. Millions have fallen prey to blind love. You are not alone.

Blind love can be corrected, but it takes a commitment to see it through. You will need the help of others who have been where you are. Don't feel upset because you can't fix your marriage by yourself. You will, without a doubt, find the answers that will enable you to fix you. Your dignity, self-esteem, self-confidence and personal happiness depend on getting help. New insight can be yours if you make a stand and take the action steps I have suggested. I guarantee the results will be eye opening.

Secret Twenty
DEALING WITH IN-LAWS

"If your in-laws were at your house every weekend, you would be angry too," Neal often complained. Neal confides to friends that his wife's parents do not give him the "space" he and his wife need. Furthermore, she doesn't seem to mind.

Neal is afraid to tell his wife how he feels, however, because he does not want to upset her or her parents. Their approval is more important to him than his own happiness.

Who is to blame for Neal's dilemma? His in-laws obviously share some blame, but he is ultimately responsible for the dissatisfaction he feels. Neal's wife is perfectly content with her parent's weekend visits. They naturally love and miss their daughter. They even grew fond of Neal.

Since Neal is the only one suffering from his in-laws' actions, should he go on ignoring his feelings? The answer is no. He could calmly discuss the matter with his wife. The two of them in turn could confront her parents. Instead, Neal seems more interested in pleasing his wife and in-laws than caring for his own needs.

Neal isn't the only one who has problems with in-laws. Lynn, a friend of mine, told a story similar to Neal's.

Lynn's in-laws supplemented her husband's income from the very first day they were married. Her in-laws helped keep their house in repair and gave them money to pay for various remodeling projects. They also gave Lynn money to buy clothes and paid for a second car she used to drive to back and forth to work.

Naturally, Lynn and her husband became dependent on his parents. This made for an uncomfortable situation.

Over time things got worse. Lynn's in-laws became intricately involved in her personal affairs as well. They interjected their unsolicited advice and asked her to explain how she budgeted her money. Lynn felt obligated to accept her in-laws' advice. All the while she secretly resented them for their meddlesome ways.

It's no wonder the day came when Lynn realized her life was no longer her own. She had enough of her in-law's money and advice. She left her husband.

Lynn admitted to her divorce recovery group that she should have put her foot down years earlier, but she was afraid her husband would not understand. She was convinced he was too dependent on his parent's support to see her side of the issue.

In truth, Lynn isn't completely innocent in the matter. She sold her marriage for material things, and bartered away her independence for economic security. Although Lynn came to realize the danger of selling herself in return for emotional and financial support, the lesson cost her dearly.

William told his support group a slightly different story. He complained that his wife's parents never really accepted him. In their opinion, he didn't make enough money or have the right kind of education. They refused to give him the approval he so desperately wanted.

Of course, William wasn't without blame. He hoped to gain a feeling of self-respect by his association with his in-laws. He mistakenly believed he was missing something and his in-laws could provide the missing piece.

William married his wife out of a sense of profound neediness and his emotional insecurity became an issue when his in-laws refused to accept him.

Linda, another friend of mine, experienced marital problems similar to William's.

Linda could not gain her in-laws acceptance either. They didn't think she was good enough for their son. He was spoiled, pampered and over indulged as a child. Linda found herself trying to replicate the care and attention his parents had given him at home. She viewed it as a challenge, a way of proving herself.

Unfortunately, Linda thought if she accomplished this lofty goal, her in-laws would accept her. Like William, Linda suffered from low self-esteem. She tied her self-worth to her relationship with her in-laws.

Millions of people complain about their in-laws when the real problem isn't their in-laws at all. The real problem is their low self-esteem.

If you are having problems with in-laws, stop and take inventory of yourself. Possibly you will discover the real reason for your dilemma. The answer to your problem is with you, *not with your in-laws*. You are responsible for your own happiness. If you have delegated responsibility to your in-laws, then you have no one to blame but yourself. You are accountable for your decision and you are the only one who can reverse it.

Does that mean you have to throw away your marriage? I think not. It does mean, however, you may have to reclaim your life and face up to your lack of self-esteem.

Are you afraid of losing the approval of your in-laws if you take such a step? If you are, remember, you have nothing to lose and everything to gain by asserting your personal rights. Neglecting to do so may result in the loss of your most cherished possession—you.

Something else you may need to do is outlaw your in-laws. You may need to put them on a visitation schedule to give you and your spouse more space. If your spouse is not agreeable to a new approach to an old problem, you may need to tell him or her how serious you are about the matter.

If your spouse values your feelings, you will no doubt work out your problem with your in-laws. However, if your spouse is still tied to mother's apron strings or dad's billfold, he or she may find it difficult to sever the ties. Then, you may have to do what is best for you. After all, you are the most important person in your world.

Making your in-laws needs more important than yours is to relegate you to a position of servitude and invite disrespect into your marriage. Possibly, that may be what you are experiencing and it may be the real reason you feel discounted and discontented.

Do you have the courage to stand up for yourself? If not, think of how you feel. The fear that haunts you is nothing more than an illusion. The misery you feel is real. It won't go away until you deal with your problem.

The examples you read about earlier all involved individuals who stood on the sidelines and watched their marriages slowly die without taking the necessary steps to reclaim their life and their spouse. What about you? Do you have what it takes to regain control of your life and your marriage? Do you have what it takes to face your problems with low self-esteem and with in-laws? I think you do. Your self-respect and personal happiness depend on it.

Secret Twenty-one
FEAR, THE ARCH ENEMY OF LOVE

Fear destroys more marriages and relationships than anything else. Fear may be the biggest single problem confronting your marriage or relationship as well.

What type of fear are we talking about? Is it the fear of heights? The fear of death? The fear of disease? The fear of darkness? The fear of old age, loss of hair, or bad luck? No, none of these. I am talking about something far more terrifying—the fear of rejection. This fear emanates from a deep sense of inferiority, shame and guilt. It causes its victims to live self-fulfilling prophecies.

Jamie enrolled in a divorce recovery group after suffering from this nagging phobia most of his life. In the safety of his support group, he admitted he felt unworthy of any woman who was pleasing and nice. He seemed to feel as if he didn't deserve anyone that good.

When Jamie married Kelly, he thought it only a matter of time before she discovered his flaws and left him for someone else. Paradoxically, fearing it made it so.

The fear of rejection caused Jamie to do strange things. He actually planned for rejection by keeping an affair with another woman going on the side. If his wife left him—he was sure she would—he had someone to turn to, an "ace in the hole," as they say.

Even when things were going well between Jamie and his wife, he ruined it by his cavalier attitude. Thinking his marriage would not last, he thought, "What's the use?" He never tried to develop a close, intimate relationship with his wife.

Divorced and with several other failed relationships to his credit, Jamie found himself searching for solutions to what seemed to be an unsolvable problem—his intense fear of rejection and the uncanny ability to make his worst fears come true.

Jamie is not alone. Carmen admitted to her support group she fears rejection, too. Carmen secretly believed she wasn't pretty enough, slender enough or smart enough to be married to someone as wonderful as Ross.

Ross was handsome, bright and successful. Although all Carmen's friends were envious of her, the fear of rejection caused her to engage in self-destructive behaviors. For example, Carmen would often work late at the office or overbook her evening appointments in an attempt to stay away from Ross. She thought if she spent too much time with him he might see her flaws and stop loving her, so she simply stayed away.

To make matters worse, Carmen refused to share her feelings with Ross. He began to think she wasn't interested in him.

Ross tried everything he knew to coax Carmen into spending more time with him. Nothing worked. Her absence stemmed from a poor self-image. A problem Ross was powerless to fix.

Ross also suffered from low self-esteem. His feelings of insecurity were intensified by Carmen's paranoia. When he realized she was not going to spend her time with him, he left her for someone who would. Carmen became the victim of her own actions.

Jean shared a somewhat different story with her support group. Jean worried incessantly about losing her husband, Tom. She envisioned him leaving her for another woman. She numbed her anxiety by binging on junk food.

Jean would stuff herself until she vomited, then remorse would set in. She would plead for Tom's forgiveness and make him promise not to leave her. He would forgive her, of course, but Jean's behavior would repeat itself a few days later.

This went on for several years until Tom grew tired of trying to quiet Jean's anxieties. He left her for someone with a heathy opinion of herself. In the final analysis, Jean experienced rejection because hidden feelings of inferiority would not allow her to accept Tom's love and support.

If the fear of rejection is the arch enemy of love, what can dispel this awful phobia? The answer is perfect love.

What is perfect love and how can you find it? How can one discern perfect love from imperfect love?

Some people never find perfect love because they don't possess the prerequisite for loving anyone else—first love yourself.

Perfect love has nothing to do with finding the right person to love you perfectly. This is a fabrication fostered by the ego. Perfect love begins with self love and extends to those around you. Without self-love, fear rushes in to fill the void, making it impossible to love or accept the love of another.

How does fear destroy your relationships? Fear, the arch enemy of love, breeds feelings of inadequacy, of not measuring up, of being less than, flawed and unworthy. These feelings motivate destructive thought patterns and, as a result, you are ultimately victimized by your own actions.

Fear of rejection prevents us from expressing anything other than paranoia, anger and worry. These negative emotions keep us from loving our spouse or anyone else because we are too absorbed in our fears. It is impossible to maintain a healthy relationship without the essential component of self-love.

If you can't find a loving relationship with another, look at your relationship with "yours truly." What do you think about yourself? What does your self-talk sound like? Does it sound demeaning or incriminating? Is the image you have of yourself a positive or negative? Do you see yourself as capable and competent or inadequate and undeserving? In short, do you love yourself?

If you do, you will feel comfortable loving someone else. Your self-confidence and self-esteem will chase away the fear of rejection and allow you to focus your undivided attention on your spouse or loved one, rather than on your fear. I call this perfect love. It is the only kind of love that will safeguard you against becoming the victim of your own actions.

Don't be too hard on yourself if your self-esteem seems shaky and your self-image isn't what it should be. Millions of people don't like themselves very much. If you find yourself in this category, here is a technique that will work for you. First, choose readings and affirmations that build self-esteem. (See Book List on page 201.) Underline every positive verse you can find. Write down the affirmations you think are especially meaningful to you on pocket size index cards and read them several times throughout the day.

Next, associate with people who are also interested in personal growth. Allow them to validate your self-esteem and help you see you deserve the best life has to offer. Let them love you. Then you love you, too. The love that casts out fear begins with you. That, my friend, is perfect love.

Secret Twenty-Two
DO YOU LOVE EACH OTHER?

Is your marriage founded on love or on something else? Countless marriages and millions of other relationships are consummated each year for reasons other than love. You can probably think of numerous reasons why love might be missing. The circumstances contributing to a loveless marriage or relationship possess several common themes.

Nancy's marriage gives insight into the circumstances keeping her from experiencing love with her husband, Matt.

Nancy enrolled in a divorce recovery group shortly after her divorce. In the safety of her support group, she admitted she knew about Matt's drinking and bouts with depression long before they were married.

Nevertheless, Nancy naively accepted his apologies and pledges after each drinking spree because she desperately wanted to believe that he would change. Matt's pathetic pleas for "one more chance," and his sad excuses played on her sympathy.

Nancy conceded she cared for Matt much like a doting mother cares for a wayward son. Matt was extremely self-centered and immature. He was attracted to Nancy because of her motherly instincts. Unfortunately, caring for someone in a maternal sense isn't the kind of love that will hold a relationship or marriage together for a lifetime.

Although she is extremely sweet, Nancy was every bit as needy as Matt. She suffered from low self-esteem, and mistakenly believed that a man would make her feel better about herself. She thought marriage would absolve her from a life of mediocrity.

After reviewing her own part in her failed marriage, Nancy realized her feelings for Matt were not rooted in love, they were rooted in the illusion he could make her feeling of inferiority go away and she could change him. Nancy also suffered from a second illusion. She believed her relationship with Matt was "special." She felt it was so special that she dare not allow him to get away because of a little problem with alcohol.

It took five years of marriage for Nancy to realize Matt wouldn't change and he couldn't be "fixed" by her. His alcoholism worsened as did her problem with low self-esteem. Instead of experiencing love, Nancy experienced a profound sense of hopelessness. She decided divorce was her only viable option.

With the help of her support group, Nancy discovered why her marriage floundered. Nancy and her husband failed at marriage because neither of them was in it for love.

Consider our second couple, Jim and Kathy.

Jim began dating Kathy even though she came with a ready-made family. Kathy's former husband was killed in a car accident ten years earlier and she was left with three small children to raise.

Jim, eight years younger than Kathy, was recently divorced and still smarting from the loss of his marriage. He found Kathy's congeniality, warmth and charm a welcome relief. She extended an open invitation to drop by anytime he wanted without calling first. An invitation Jim took her up on regularly.

It wasn't long before Jim began spending week nights with Kathy. As the months went by, their relationship intensified—at least in Kathy's mind.

All went well for several more months, then Kathy asked Jim for a commitment. Although he was fond of Kathy, Jim was reluctant to commit to a woman with children and he made up an excuse to put Kathy off for the time being.

Another four or five months passed and Kathy again approached Jim about a commitment. This time, however, Jim told Kathy how he felt. She was outraged. She demanded that he leave and never darken her doorstep again. Jim left.

After several days went by, his insecurity grew and he decided to reconsider Kathy's demands and call her. After he groveled on the phone for several minutes, Kathy took Jim back on condition that he buy her an engagement ring. He agreed and their relationship continued. This time the stakes were much higher.

More time elapsed. The engagement ring failed to materialize. Kathy pressured Jim about the ring and threatened to call off their engagement if it didn't appear soon. Jim again agreed to Kathy's demands and a ring was purchased.

Four or five more months passed and Kathy popped the big question. "When will we get married?" she asked. Jim, still frightened of marriage, pleaded for more time to plan for their wedding date. Kathy, remembering that he had come around to her demands in the past, assumed that a date would be set.

Meanwhile, Jim left town on a business trip. When he returned, he went to his house instead of Kathy's. Kathy called Jim and asked him why he hadn't come over. He informed her their relationship was finished and he would not be seeing her anymore.

Unbeknownst to Kathy, Jim had been cultivating a relationship with a co-worker who "just happened" to accompany him on his trip. In the friendly confines of his hotel room, he consummated his new affair.

Kathy fell into deep depression. "What went wrong?" she demanded.

After sharing her story with her support group, the answers became clear. Kathy wanted a man in her life, someone to be a father to her children. Jim was lonely and he saw Kathy as someone who would care for him, nurse him back to emotional health and stick by his side until he felt strong enough to move to another relationship. Jim and Kathy were a perfect fit because neither of them was in it for love.

Ted and Martha were married right out of high school. Within five years they were the parents of two darling little boys. They went to church together and both had good jobs.

To all outward appearances Ted and Martha looked like devout Christians, responsible parents and the perfect couple. Looks are deceiving, as Martha explained later. The image Ted projected in public was quite different from the image he projected when they were alone.

"Ted was a Christian," Martha said, but he intensely disliked church. He only went because she made him. While at church, Ted pretended to be the model husband. It was a very different story at home. Ted was never around. He was involved in recreational sports and played on a different softball team every night of the week.

Martha would often get angry with Ted for spending his evenings with the guys. She knew he had to go to work the next morning. Besides, the kids missed him when he was gone.

Martha finally confronted Ted about his irresponsible behavior. In response, he quietly packed some things and moved in with a single friend who played on one of his softball teams. This marked the beginning of the end for Martha's marriage.

She tried to explain to her support group how wonderful her marriage was until Ted started hanging around his friend. Martha even went so far as to call Ted an outstanding Christian who loved his children and worked hard to provide for their needs—that is until his friend entered their lives. Fortunately, Martha's support group saw through her denial. What Martha really meant was that she enjoyed feeling in control, until Ted ran away from home. Even then, she blamed his friend and exonerated Ted of all responsibility for his actions.

Ted was immature, to be sure. He wanted someone to take charge, but he eventually grew tired of Martha's domineering ways and decided to test his wings and fly on his own.

Martha finally figured out what went wrong. Neither she nor her husband was in the marriage for love.

I could go on with more examples, but the preceding stories illustrate how a person can feel stuck in a marriage or relationship without being in love. Unfortunately, basing either on anything other than love will only result in pain and heartache.

How about you? If you are in a marriage or relationship for any other reason besides love, it's time for you to admit it. Tell a close confidant, such as a counselor, a friend or your minister. Ask them to hear you out. Confess your motives and reveal your fears. Then take inventory of your marriage or relationship.

Ask yourself if the assets outweigh the liabilities. If they do, there is hope. If not, then you need to seek a support group to help you work out your problem with dignity and common sense. A therapist or experienced friend can point you to the group right for you. Love is the only bond strong enough to hold a marriage or relationship together for a lifetime.

Secret Twenty-Three
THE ROOT CAUSE OF STRIFE

Are you concerned about the arguments, conflicts, discord, infidelity, dissension, friction, turmoil and abuse in your marriage? Hatred is a chief cause of strife. Fear, resentment, and feelings of hostility are the negative emotions that produce hatred.

Why would a person feel fearful, angry and hostile? Often, it is because of some form of emotional or physical abandonment in the past. Perhaps he or she was sexually, emotionally or physically abused as a child. Neglect, rejection or unfair criticism by parents, teachers, or friends can leave scars on the psyche.

Whatever the case, these are the kinds of experiences that leave people feeling resentful, hostile, and fearful of people for the rest of their lives. Painful memories associated with these negative experiences have a way of reappearing at the most inopportune time to spoil your most treasured relationships—particularly marriage.

When innocuous comments are taken out of context, blown out of proportion or trigger a fit of rage for no apparent reason, the innocent bystander is left wondering, "What happened?"

What happened was that hurt feelings from the past were triggered. This launched a tirade of unflattering words and malicious acts aimed at getting even for the perceived wrong. In reality, a festering wound touched off an emotional explosion far more intense than called for by the present situation. A person's personal history forms a powerful link to present day events. Hatred, evolving from past events, can seize the moment without the slightest warning.

It doesn't stop there. A second way in which the past haunts the future is through the dangerous practice of projection. By projecting a specific outcome, situation or event, one can create either positive or negative results. It works like this: When your spouse says or does something that reminds you of a painful memory from the past, you may mistakenly project an outcome similar to what you experienced previously—one you will do anything to avoid.

If the outcome was unpleasant, as it surely was, your ego defenses are activated in an attempt to elude the anticipated event. As a result, you scare yourself into an inappropriate reaction, thereby contributing to the very circumstances you fear most.

I personally believe infidelity is often one spouse's attempt to counterbalance a feeling of rejection or abandonment by the other—a feeling based on some negative memory from the past. A case in point is the spouse whose sexual advances are rebuffed. He or she may interpret the rebuff as rejection. If they do, they may think their spouse is no longer interested in them sexually, and look elsewhere to validate their self-esteem.

Sometimes a spouse may feel neglected, ignored or abandoned if their wife or husband is frequently gone. These negative feelings are commonly associated with the workaholic spouse. They, too, may lead to infidelity if feelings trigger negative memories.

Those who find themselves entangled in extramarital affairs probably would not explain their behavior the way I have. They would tell you something is missing in their marriage and they are seeking the missing ingredient in someone else.

What is missing? The kind of love that will forgive all wrongs, real and imagined, past and present.

A love that covers all sins doesn't deny what happened in the past. It simply sees today's events and circumstances for what they are—present day problems. Love deals with them, then moves on.

"My past was so painful I don't think I could ever forgive or forget what happened," you may be thinking. Fear not! There is a solution, but to activate it requires forgiveness.

"Forgive? Who, me?" you ask. Yes, you. Although you were the one who was wronged, you hold the key to the solution. It may seem to be too much to handle, but I am going to reveal the secret about what really happened to you.

The secret is that whatever happened in the past, or for that matter the present, was not about you. It was a reflection of the mental, emotional or spiritual condition of the person or persons who wronged you. They have the problem, not you. Forgive them, whoever they are, for their souls are troubled, too. Realizing it was not about you but about them should be a freeing thought and also a comforting truth.

Remember this truth as well. Anger and hostility will only keep you tied to the past. Forgiveness will free you from it. Love and forgiveness can replace animosity and hostility if you use this secret to your advantage. It is the only way you will ever experience the kind of love that will free you from the past and insure positive results in the future.

Allow me to close this secret with a positive thought and a personal affirmation that will help you to come to terms with your past and live in the present.

"Whatever things are true, whatever things are honest, whatever things are just, whatever things are pure, whatever things are lovely, whatever things are of good report; think of these things."

These are the thoughts of love. Begin thinking them. Keep your mind focused on these thoughts and your attitude will soon become positive. Positive thoughts lead to happiness in life and happiness in love.

Recite this affirmation with me: *"Today, I will lay aside every painful memory and hurtful resentment that torments me. I will live with love and patience the life laid before me."*

Repeat this affirmation once in the morning and again before bedtime for the next twenty-one days and watch strife disappear from your life. I promise you the results will amaze you.

Secret Twenty-Four
AWE-STRUCK

Elizabeth met Will in college. She dreamed of becoming a successful attorney. He had his sights set on becoming a surgeon.

Although Elizabeth's intelligence matched or surpassed Will's, she seemed in awe of him. Will was not only tall, handsome and charming, but he came from a well-to-do family. He drove a flashy sports car, owned an impressive wardrobe and always had plenty of money. Elizabeth swore she would do everything in her power to win him.

She changed her hairstyle. She began to dress differently. Next, she adopted a pretentious attitude and acquiesced to Will's sexual advances hoping to hold his interest. Something else happened as well. Elizabeth slacked off on her own studies so she could help Will cram for exams.

Through it all, Elizabeth somehow managed to finish law school. She secured a position with a small law firm. All the while, she continued to see Will.

This went on until Will began his internship. He asked Elizabeth to marry him. She accepted and within a few months they were married.

Will opened up a medical practice. He asked Elizabeth to resign her position at the law firm so she could help him establish his office. She agreed.

Success came fast for Will. An extravagant lifestyle followed, replete with memberships to swank clubs and acceptance into the city's highest circles of society.

In the process, Elizabeth lost herself in Will's achievements. In her mind, life seemed grand. However, Will was leading a double life.

Will began staying away from home more. He told Elizabeth that he had to work harder to maintain their standard of living. Elizabeth didn't seem to mind. She liked being known as Doctor Will's wife and she was enjoying the fruits of his labor. She continued to manage his office and oversee his growing practice.

One day, Elizabeth's storybook marriage began to unravel. Will failed to come home after making his evening rounds at the hospital.

Elizabeth had grown accustomed to her husband's late hours. He would sometimes arrive home at three or four in the morning with a tale about a sick patient who needed his attention in the emergency room. However, this morning was different. Will was nowhere to be found.

Elizabeth called the hospital. She checked with friends to no avail. Late the next day he called. Speaking briefly from a pay phone, Will told Elizabeth in no uncertain terms their marriage was over. He told her he had fallen in love with another woman and his attorney would be in touch.

Elizabeth felt disbelief and shock. Panic gripped her, then denial. Sadly, it was all too true. As she relayed her story to the others in her divorce recovery group, emotions ran high. Elizabeth wept as she shared how she immersed herself in her husband's life and he left her with nothing. All the years she invested in him and his career were gone. She felt betrayed. "What went wrong?" Elizabeth asked.

The answer is obvious. Elizabeth was awe-struck, not love-struck, as she presumed. The very moment Elizabeth met Will, she proclaimed him wiser and more capable than herself. She assumed someday he would be an outstanding success without daring to envision similar good fortune for herself. Elizabeth's self-worth had become so intertwined with her husband's accomplishments that she lost her own identity.

How about you? Are you awe-struck or love-struck?

The awe-struck person assumes the other person is smarter, better looking and more capable. Those who are awe-struck often abdicate their personal rights to the other person by placing them on a pedestal and heralding them as their "savior." Worst of all, awe-struck precedes the loss of self-worth and self-confidence,

Love-struck is another matter altogether. Love-struck assumes equality. When you are love-struck, you are not "making believe" the other person is more intelligent, better looking or more capable than you. Love-struck encourages individuality and the attainment of the highest goals.

The natural defense against feeling awe-struck is that you will never become awe-struck as long as you love and respect yourself as much as you do the other person. Love who you are and what you are. Love yourself so much that you never surrender your identity to anyone else.

Be who you are and become all you were meant to be. Find and live your life's purpose, not that of someone else. The pleasure of being love-struck awaits you when you do.

Secret Twenty-Five
SECRETS

Marsha had a secret. When she was a junior in high school, she had sex with a young man and became pregnant. Her parents were outraged. They berated her day and night, telling her that she shamed the family name and that anyone who slept around was a "slut."

Marsha's parents were so embarrassed they took her out of school and moved to another town. There they found a doctor to abort Marsh's pregnancy.

After the abortion, Marsha enrolled in a new school. Her parents forbade her to talk about the incident. Marsha lived with her secret through college and continued to live with it until she married Phil several years after graduation.

A year into marriage, Phil began making overtures about having children. When Marsha heard this, her secret reared its ugly head. Overwhelmed by guilt and shame, she refused to discuss the matter. The memories associated with her secret were too painful to deal with.

Not one to give up, Phil tried repeatedly to talk to Marsha about starting a family, only to discover she had become depressed over the issue. Finally, after unrelenting pressure from Phil, Marsha admitted she had a secret. Much to her surprise, he understood the power of secrets. They worked through her past together. Today they are the proud parents of twins.

Robin also failed to tell her husband about her secret. Robin had been married before. The marriage lasted less than a year and she pushed it out of her mind, hoping never to tell anyone.

Things were fine until an old girlfriend of Robin's called one evening. William answered the phone. The voice on the line called him Chad, a name he had not heard before. William corrected the young lady and she apologized for her mistake, but his curiosity had been aroused.

William asked Robin about Chad but she brushed him off. Unsatisfied with her answer, William continued to prod Robin until she revealed her secret. Luckily William understood and Robin's secret lost its power to hurt her marriage.

Rhonda also failed to tell her husband, Mitch, about her secret. Rhonda had been sexually abused as a child. Because of feelings of shame and guilt, she kept the secret from Mitch and her family.

Everything seemed normal between Rhonda and Mitch until she began refusing his sexual advances. Rhonda explained that she was not in the mood and didn't feel well. Mitch said he understood.

This went on for several months. Finally, Mitch persuaded Rhonda to see a counselor. In the safety of the counselor's office, Rhonda revealed why she could not be physically intimate with her husband. Fortunately, the two of them cared enough about their marriage to face her secret together. Today they are one of the happiest couples you will ever meet.

Tammy had a secret, too. Although raised in a devout Christian home, she had a sexual encounter with another female student when she was a freshman in college. The other girl, a junior, persuaded Tammy that the whole thing was nothing more than an experiment. However, Tammy carried the secret with her for the next three years.

After graduation, Tammy met a man named Robert. Tammy liked Robert and wanted to tell him about her secret but she was too afraid. She thought he would stop seeing her if he knew. Like her parents, he was a devout Christian.

Instead of telling Robert, Tammy told a friend at work.

The "friend" used the information to sabotage Tammy's chances for a promotion. When Tammy found out about the betrayal, she resigned.

Ashamed and confused, she went into isolation and refused to return Robert's calls. Their relationship seemed over—except Robert would not give up. Realizing Tammy's behavior was out of character, he attempted to see her. He waited outside her apartment until she appeared and then he confronted her. Robert assured Tammy he loved her knew she wasn't acting like herself. He said, judging by her behavior, she needed help.

Together they agreed to seek counseling. In therapy, Tammy unloaded her secret. Today, Tammy and Robert are happily married.

Secrets come in many forms. Those who bury their secrets hoping they will never be revealed are usually too terrified of rejection to share them. Our examples showed that isn't what happens many times. The problem with secrets is that the person with the secret feels too ashamed to come clean. Their shame promotes a feeling of separation, which in turn causes them to act inappropriately.

Do you have a secret? Don't wait for your spouse to find out. Don't fool yourself; he or she will find out. It's only a matter of time. It may take six months or six years but your secret will come out.

Hopefully, you have the desire to rid yourself of your secret. The old saying goes, "We are as sick as our secrets."

Secrets make you emotionally, mentally and spiritually ill because they separate you from those who could love you the most. A secret is a burden too heavy to bear alone. The effects can be disastrous, not only on your marriage, but on you as well.

Unfortunately, most people believe their secrets are small, inconsequential and harmless. But are they? Secrets cause problems no matter how small they seem. Maybe you have an incident in your past you have decided to keep secret. Possibly, you are acting in a way that is destructive to your relationship or marriage. Is your secret the reason for your behavior? If so, then I have a question for you. Have you ever wondered how secrets are born? Secrets evolve out of a deep wound to your self-esteem which prevents you from liking yourself. You are unable to envision how anyone else could like you either. The part of your personality that you find objectionable becomes the source of your secret. You spend your time and energy trying to cover it up. Your secret is what separates you from those who would love you if only you would let them.

The underlying problem is self-hatred and self-loathing, not the secret. The good news is that your secret isn't unique. Others have had the same secret, or one much worse. Take my advice. Get rid of your secret.

Perhaps you shouldn't confess your secret to your spouse. Possibly you need to confess your secret to a therapist, counselor, minister, priest, rabbi or spiritual confidant.

You may need to look your secret square in the eyes and denounce it as a lie. You may need to command those secret feelings of inadequacy and inferiority to leave forever. *You* must decide the proper way to unload a secret that is driving you crazy and threatening your marriage or relationship.

Make your choice wisely. If you release the secret by confessing it to someone worthy of your trust, you will find much needed healing for your self-esteem. The healing comes from a clear conscience, a feeling of belonging and the knowledge that your secret is not unique.

Secret Twenty-Six
THE PROBLEM WITH JEALOUSY

Love is not a part of jealousy. Love thrives on trust, while jealousy thrives on doubt.

Ted conceded to the others in his divorce recovery group that he once thought of jealousy as a healthy emotion. Ted would feel jealous whenever his wife looked at another man or, God forbid, talked to him for any length of time. Jealousy represented an outward sign of an innermost feeling called love to Ted. He saw nothing wrong with jealousy, even though fear and anger always accompanied this dark emotion.

His jealousy provoked thoughts such as, "She wants him, not me." "She doesn't look at me that way." "She isn't that talkative when it's just the two of us." "Why is she standing so close to him?" "Why is she sitting next to him and not me?"

Jealousy would overwhelm Ted and he would say something inappropriate, especially if he had been drinking. Statements such as, "You really want him, don't you?" "Why don't you talk to me the way you talk to him?" And, "Why don't you look at me the way you look at him?"

For some inexplicable reason, Ted couldn't figure out why his accusatory remarks insulted his wife. The repercussions didn't stop there. Ted's wife interpreted his caustic remarks as an affront to her integrity. It seemed Ted had offended her for no apparent reason.

Ted's jealous behavior was personally humiliating as well. Feeling inferior and fearing abandonment, it was obvious he lacked self-confidence.

When Ted exhibited a jealous attitude, his wife found him repulsive and often told him so.

Ted's accusations were self-incriminating, too. He was secretly considering having an affair. He subconsciously projected his treasonous thoughts onto his wife.

After discussing his failed marriage with his divorce recovery group, Ted began to understand how incredulous his jealous assertions must have sounded to his innocent wife. Just as importantly, he recognized the error in his thinking and why he entertained such absurd thoughts in the first place.

Here are some lessons Ted learned.

To begin with, love requires trust. Trust is an integral part of any successful marriage or relationship. Ted's jealousy revealed his mistrust in the one person he professed to love the most—his wife. Ted's mistrust also indicated a lack of confidence and deep insecurity in the one person Ted's wife loved most—Ted.

Ted's jealousy eventually convinced his wife of the very thing he seemed convinced of himself. He was inadequate, inferior and undeserving of her love.

In time, Ted's wife began to realize what she shared with him wasn't love, or else why would he genuinely mistrust her? The impersonal demon known as jealousy, buoyed by the dreadful fear of abandonment, finally ruined Ted's marriage. It happened when he allowed jealousy to dominate his thoughts and control his behavior.

Can you see why love demands trust and how jealousy will destroy a relationship? Before you can trust another, you must trust yourself. This requires a healthy degree of self-esteem and self-confidence. Self-esteem and self-confidence in turn create an environment where love can flourish.

Trust is a belief that starts with yourself and extends to the one you love. Trust equals faith—faith in yourself, in your spouse, in your relationship and in your marriage.

Secondly, a love that trusts is unselfish. A love that trusts isn't concerned about what it will lose. It is, however, deeply concerned with what it can give.

Ted was fearful he would end up alone. He wasn't thinking of anyone but himself. Jealousy is always motivated by "me first" thinking, while trust is rooted in a spirit of benevolence.

Third, a love that trusts is liberating. A love that trusts asks for volunteers, while jealousy takes captives.

Last, a love that trusts demands honesty. Jealousy thrives on deceit. Ted practiced deception in his marriage and his wife eventually grew tired of his attempts to manipulate the truth.

If jealousy is flirting with your emotions, spend time rereading this secret. Use it as an affirmation and replace jealousy with faith, unselfishness, trust and honesty. Your relationship will never be the same if you do.

Secret Twenty-Seven
DREAMS AND PROMISES

The familiar 50s tune entitled, *Love Me Tender* is a favorite of mine. The reason probably has as much to do with my affinity for the famous singer who recorded this nostalgic classic as it does to its beautiful refrain, "Love me tender, love me true, all my dreams fulfill, for my darling I love you, and I always will."

As I began to think about the magic in this well known chorus, I discovered two positively alluring ideas, both of which can be found in romantic literature the world over.

The first idea promotes the false hope that another person, namely someone of the opposite sex, can make our every dream come true. The other is the appealing yet naive idea that love can be promised to another forever—"and I always will"—as if that is all there is to it.

How many of you have secretly longed for Prince Charming or Cinderella to suddenly appear and make all your dreams come true? Who hasn't pledged their allegiance to another, hoping to seal their affection with a single promise, only to watch love die like a smoldering ember?

Maybe you are married to someone you thought would make all your dreams come true. Or you vowed to love each other "till death do you part." Then, for whatever reason, you end up feeling disappointed, sad, and alone. The majority of participants in divorce recovery groups mistakenly believed these erroneous ideas and had their hearts broken.

Why is the chorus to *Love Me Tender* both romantic and dangerous? From my experience, it is painfully

117

obvious that when you make someone else responsible for your dreams, you are setting yourself up to become the victim.

You know the definition of a victim. A victim in a relationship is often one who has a leaning, dependent personality. They are the pathetic, appalling persons who eventually lose the love and respect of those closest to them. They experience rejection and loneliness without ever knowing why.

Please believe me when I tell you another human being cannot make your dreams come true. The responsibility for achieving your highest ideals is yours, and yours alone, no matter whom you married.

Lylia, an acquaintance of mine, recalled her days in college. As a student, she dreamed of working in Europe and traveling to exciting places. Lylia's dream was unexpectedly interrupted when her boyfriend, John, asked her to marry him.

Lylia liked John, maybe she even loved him—she wasn't quite sure. She was sure of one thing, however. John was the only man who had ever shown any real interest in her.

Lylia thought, can I afford to lose him? Maybe a college degree and living in Europe are unrealistic goals. Perhaps I should marry John and settle down, she reasoned.

To help Lylia with her decision, John promised to take her on a vacation to Europe some day. He also promised her a big home with beautiful furniture and all the comforts a woman could want. Lylia was persuaded. She accepted John's proposal and they were married the next spring.

Twenty years later, Lylia wept as she told me how she threw away her dream of working and traveling across Europe when she agreed to marry John. "What happened to my dream and the deal we made?" she wondered.

Lylia made the mistake many people make. She thought the person she married could compensate her for sacrificing her dreams.

Lylia lived in a fabulous house all right, but it was not a home. She also had plenty of money but it could not buy happiness. She even enjoyed a life of leisure but she didn't have love. Lylia's husband was a workaholic and his career became his obsession. He eventually fell in love with a co-worker and Lylia had nothing, not even her dream.

Why are dreams important? When you lose your dream you lose yourself—the one person you can't afford to live without.

There's good news. Lylia realized the error in her thinking. She went back to college and graduated with a teaching degree. After a short stint at a local school, she moved to Europe where she teaches American children who accompany their parents on assignment from the U.S. State Department.

Oh yes, Lylia eventually remarried but this time it is different. She is living her dream.

Remember the second popular notion found in the unforgettable chorus to *Love Me Tender*? It suggests we can somehow pledge our love to another and never have to worry about it again. Although the idea sounds good, it doesn't hold up in actual experience. Terry and Janet are a case in point.

Terry courted Janet for nearly two years before he finally won her heart. As soon as Janet finished college, Terry asked her to marry him. She accepted and seven months later they were married.

Meanwhile, the U.S. economy went into a deep recession. Without warning Terry lost his job. Although he subsequently found work, his salary was half of what he was previously making. Janet had to shoulder most of the financial burdens.

Something else was different, too. Terry and Janet began focusing their attention on their problems and ignored each other. It seemed to them they had to worry about school loans, a better job, insurance coverage, car repairs and a variety of other things. There would be time for each other once their problems were behind them. For now, all of that would have to wait.

This went on for nearly three years and Janet finally had enough. Unable to bear up under the financial strain and feeling unloved and lonely, she left Terry and filed for divorce. Janet had fallen out of love with Terry because he turned his attention to the cares of life and neglected his relationship with her.

Terry and Janet made a classic mistake. They falsely assumed love was settled once and for all when they exchanged "I do's." Like so many others, they labored under the illusion that their relationship was secondary in importance to other issues.

Here are some tips to help you avoid losing your relationship to the cares of life.

► Don't allow yourself to get too far in debt.
► Don't make your job your life.
► Be sure to make time for each other during the day.
► Hug a lot.
► Talk a lot.
► Say, "I love you," often.
► Listen to each other.
► Help each other.
► Attend church or synagogue together.
► Get involved in a mutual interest of some kind.
► Designate one evening a week as date night.

Here are some tips that will help you and your spouse live your dream.

► Define your dream.
► Define the steps you plan to take to achieve your

dream.

- Communicate your dream to each other.
- Define how your dream will benefit you and your spouse.
- Identify how you will share the benefits with others.
- Clearly see yourself as having achieved your dream and enjoying the benefits.
- Decide when you will begin working toward your dream.
- Set a date for accomplishing it.

Use these helpful tips to give your marriage dreams that will last a lifetime.

Secret Twenty-Eight
WRONG IDEAS

What would you say if someone told you you may be living with wrong ideas about God, yourself and other people? What would you say if that same person told you your faulty concepts may be causing problems in your marriage or relationship?

Hanna fit this category. She came to her divorce recovery group with lots of erroneous ideas. Little wonder she seemed angry, depressed and confused. Fortunately, Hanna opened up to her support group and her mood began to change.

As Hanna told her story it became clear her parents were an inferiority riddled, hard working, middle class couple who struggled to make ends meet. In Hanna's words, they were up to their eyeballs in debt because they insisted on living as their "friends" did.

Although, Hanna's mother and father worked for a fortune 500 company, neither achieved much success in their chosen careers. Frustrated and resentful, they took particular pleasure in "bad mouthing" anyone who earned more money, lived in a nicer house or drove a newer car than they did.

"If you had a jerk for a boss, you would be angry, too," Hanna's father would say.

"At least you don't have to work with a bunch of brown nose, no-account, lazy so and sos," Hanna's mother would counter.

"Why did we even bother going to college? Office politics and 'buttering up' the boss are the only things that count," they moaned.

They often repeated the familiar refrain that fate had dealt them a bad hand. So much so that Hanna wondered why they had not been given the same material blessings that others enjoyed.

Hanna's parents convinced themselves they were destined to live lives of quiet desperation. Their belief was compounded by their faulty concept of God. They envisioned God as an authoritarian despot who meted out favors to a chosen few and neglected the rest of humanity out of sheer spite. They described Him as, "the Old Man up stairs" with little or no interest in what went on down here. They were sure He had no interest in them or their plight.

Hanna learned her parents' pessimistic attitude. She mastered the comparison game and felt unworthy of the good things in life.

Through it all, Hanna's parents said they wanted the best for her. They must have told Hanna a thousand times that one day Mr. Right would come along and rescue her from a life of toil and woe.

Hanna felt sure the man she ultimately married was the Mr. Right of whom her parents often spoke. Hanna secretly felt unworthy of his love, but she married him anyway, hoping he would sooth her feelings of inferiority.

During the marriage, Hanna secretly worried that her husband, Edward, would one day leave her for someone younger, smarter or better looking.

Hanna began living for her husband's approval. She thought if she could keep him happy, he would not have a legitimate reason to leave her. She worked feverishly and spent lavishly on him trying to make his life as comfortable as possible. She bought him the latest fashions, made it possible for him to drive an expensive sports car and purchase a lake recreational home for weekend getaways. He also spent money on a personal trainer, a fancy ski boat, jet skies and other popular gadgets of the day. He hired someone to do light maintenance around the house so he would not have to work when he got home from the office.

Hanna didn't realize it, but her husband was needy, too. He also came from a dysfunctional family. His parents were workaholics who emotionally abandoned him and withheld their love. Hanna's husband was incapable of loving anyone, including himself. She described him as a "bottomless pit" who couldn't be satisfied or show love and approval no matter what she did.

Five years after they were married, Hanna and her husband had accumulated more debt than they could possibly pay off on their incomes alone. Echoing her parents, she complained about their misfortune and compared herself to her friends and co-workers. She was also blaming God for their predicament and her attitude became more negative each day. As Hanna's attitude changed, so did her husband's.

He became depressed over their financial problems. It wasn't long before he began having an affair with another woman. Hanna found out and confronted him. Rather than deny it, he walked out, never to return. Now Hanna had someone else to blame for her troubles—the other woman.

Luckily, the participants in Hanna's divorce recovery group helped her gain a new perspective of herself and her marriage. Hanna discovered her personal power by taking responsibility for her mistaken beliefs and confronting the devastating effect they had on her marriage. Eventually, Hanna began to see she was not the helpless victim she liked to portray herself as. She was, in fact, part of the problem and her own worst enemy.

Hanna believed she was undeserving and unworthy of the good things in life. She unwittingly married a man who was sure to prove her right. Mr. Right *was* right for Hanna. Hanna convinced herself she would never have the good things in life. Mr. Right was who she needed because he was incapable of giving them to her.

With more time in recovery, Hanna eventually began to see she was equipped with everything she would ever need to succeed.

Hanna's self image improved. She stopped playing the comparison game and no longer felt inadequate. Oh yes, Hanna eventually met and married Rob. This marriage is different. Hanna now knows she deserves the best.

What are your beliefs? Like Hanna, most of our beliefs are formed during childhood. Shame-based parents infect their children with attitudes like, "What's the use" and "I haven't got a chance" the same way a contagious disease is transmitted from one unsuspecting person to another. Parents pass along the rules to the comparison game and its companion attitudes of, "You are not as good as. . . What makes you think you can . . . ?" And, "God obviously does not care as much for you as he does for others."

It's no wonder the person who believes they are inferior hears an inner voice saying at the most inopportune time, "Look at her, she is more beautiful, more intelligent and more deserving than you are, what makes you think you could ever be like her and have what she has?" This negative self-talk reinforces mistaken beliefs.

Unless you are willing to discover and discard unworkable ideas, your personal happiness will remain far below an acceptable level. Chances of achieving success in life, marriage, or relationships will be poor.

Do what Hanna did. Examine your belief system. Look into your past. What did you hear at home? What did you learn from your parents or other trusted caregivers? How did those beliefs influence your life? How did they influence your marriage or relationship? You can reverse and correct the harmful effects the past is having on you, your life and your marriage. Hanna did it and so can you.

Secret Twenty-Nine
BE CAREFUL WHAT YOU HEAR

If you hear the good things that are said, more good things will be given to you to hear—positive statements that build warm relationships, self-esteem and personal confidence.

However, if you allow your ears to pervert what is being said into something that sounds demeaning or threatening, the little good you previously heard will be taken from you, leaving you worse off than before.

A personal story illustrates my point: I remember an incident that took place several years ago. My wife tried to share a bit of helpful information about a dinner party we were planning to attend. She stated she had talked to Mrs. Smith (who was also planning to attend the party) who said that Mr. Smith (who I knew to be young and quite successful) was going to be wearing a sport shirt, khaki pants and tan loafers to the party we were invited to attend.

An innocent comment, would you agree? Wrong. I heard, "Mr. Smith is wearing really 'cool' clothes. Don't embarrass me by dressing like a nerd. Try to dress like Mr. Smith. Maybe then you will be 'cool' too."

Are you thinking, "How in the world did he twist his wife's comment into a threatening message like that?"

How? My poor self-esteem and profound insecurity impaired my ability to hear what was really being said. I interpreted my wife's remark to mean I was socially inept, personally unappealing and inferior when compared to Mr. Smith.

I would counter with a remark such as, "Who does Mr. Smith think he is anyway? What makes him the expert in fashion? Who made him the standard for desirability?

Would you prefer that I looked like Mr. Smith? Would you rather be married to him than to me?"

Next, I turned my exaggerating mind to other occasions when my wife may have made similar comments. Did I embarrass her then, too? What about my manners? Did she find them offensive as well? Was she secretly thinking the other men present were more desirable, more handsome or more "hip" than me?

My suspicious mind searched my memory trying to determine whether past remarks made by my wife were as disparaging as the ones I *thought* I heard her make now. Continuing in this ridiculous mode, I usually decided they had been every bit as disparaging, but I had naively overlooked them at the time.

My talent for rewriting history destroyed or invalidated memories I had of past events. Memories that may have been thoroughly delightful until my faulty hearing ruined them for both me and my wife.

Janice told her divorce recovery group a similar story. She said her ex-husband, Sam, threw a horrendous fit whenever she dared mention Bill, the husband of her best friend Debbie.

Bill was a tall, good-looking man in his early 30s who owned his own business. Janice's husband, Sam, was in his mid 40s and stuck in a dead-end job. He twisted Janice's comments to mean he was somehow inferior to Bill. Sam eventually forbid Janice to see Debbie.

As time went on, he also prohibited her from seeing other friends whose husbands were doing well in their careers. This continued until Janice finally had enough and left Sam. His "hearing problem" destroyed his marriage, leaving him in worse condition than before.

Another example is Carl. He was in his mid 40s, married to a woman in her early 30s. Since he worked as the lead anchor for a local television station, his wife would often say something such as, "It must be interesting to work with Mr. Jones. As the sports director, he must meet some really famous people. What does he say about Tiger Woods?"

Carl would instantly explode with anger. He would scold his wife, telling her sports directors were nothing more than over-the-hill jocks who could not do anything else for a living. Then he would chide her for assuming Mr. Jones was an interesting person. Carl's wife would be silent for several days, afraid to say anything more about the subject.

Invariably, however, she would ask about other personalities. Carl's suspicious mind would go to work, misinterpreting his wife's remarks to mean she was interested in the weather man, the beat reporter or whoever she happened to ask about.

After several years, Carl's wife divorced him.

Later, Carl conceded to his divorce recovery group that he had distorted his wife's statements and rejected her love and attention all because of an acute "hearing problem." As in our other example, the relationship Carl had was destroyed by him, leaving him in worse straits than before.

Millions of people have hearing problems—the kind that can't be corrected with a hearing aid. Their problem stems from feelings of low self-esteem, a poor self-image and a lack of self-confidence, all of which leads them to distort what is being said, twist it into something demeaning. They respond inappropriately, leaving them with more problems with which to contend.

Sometimes, even if what is really being said sounds good, they misinterpret and discredit it. If the remark sounds bad, they embellish it. Always expecting rejection, they are seldom disappointed.

What does it take to correct a "hearing problem?"

First, as with all problem solving, you must realize and accept you have the problem before the healing process can begin.

Second, you must work at filling your mind with good thoughts and honorable intentions where your spouse is concerned.

Last, you must work at putting a positive spin on your spouse's comments by recasting them in a more favorable light.

When my mind is saturated with positive thoughts about my wife, I hear love in her voice and feel revered when I'm with her. I behave like the warm, gentle person that I am. Then, I receive the love and admiration my self-esteem needs.

When I hear affirming messages in my wife's statements, good is given back to me. It can happen to you when you correct your "hearing problem."

Secret Thirty
MONEY PROBLEMS

Marriage counselors will tell you money problems destroy more marriages than anything else.

A well-known Bible verse identifies, "The love of money as the root of all evil." If you feel your problems are related to money, think again. The basis of your problem may be the love of money.

Is money the number one priority in your life? You may be so enamored with money it has become your higher power. You may be worshiping the almighty green back rather than God.

What happens when you fall in love with money? You eventually experience many sorrows. The major sorrow is bankruptcy. However, most of us are solvent, though sometimes, barely.

How about you? Do you live from paycheck to paycheck? Are you over your head in debt? Are you living with a house payment that stretches your financial resources each month? Are you paying for expensive cars, clothes or other things and feeling the financial stress of trying to live like the "Jones family?"

Why do people live paycheck to paycheck and spend Their hard earned money on everything under the sun? They think the more they have, the happier they will be. Especially if they have all the proverbial "Joneses" have.

Unfortunately, money can't buy happiness and the Jones family is probably trying to keep up with the Smiths. Both may be living on the brink of financial disaster.

Another reason people find themselves in financial difficulty is the easy availability of credit cards. The capacity to multiply monthly income gives them a false sense of empowerment.

Some people turn to credit cards and home equity loans when they feel powerless to change circumstances in their life they find objectionable. Spending money becomes a way to get even, or to act out unresolved anger, frustration and disappointment. A credit card or line of credit makes them feel powerful in an otherwise powerless situation.

You don't have to be a victim of impulse. You can control your thoughts and choose to view the people and circumstances in your life in a different light. You can discover personal power and it won't cost you a dime. You can understand that although you can't change the people, places or things bothering you, you can change your reaction to them.

Another way people get themselves into trouble after falling in love with money is mistakenly believing money means status. Money becomes a symbol of success that elicits good "vibes." The more money they have, the more successful they feel.

This leads to yet another problem for some people. They become so obsessed with making money they neglect their family and their health. All the while, they feel as if they never have enough money no matter how much they make and no matter how hard they work.

These are the people who become workaholics. They spend more time and energy trying to make money than they do trying to build a meaningful relationship with their wife and children. Although there may be a pot of gold at the end of the rainbow, gold can't buy back their family or health once they are gone.

Don't be fooled by people you meet at the other side of the rainbow. Those who gather around pots of gold are not really your friends. They are not worth the sacrifice of your family and health.

The idea that money equals security is the final reason

you fall in love with money and experience heartache in the process.

People who save a lot of money in an attempt to compound its value and build a net worth to make themselves secure later in life must be careful not to become misers and penny pinchers who sacrifice their family's short-term happiness.

"Tighten the belt today and reap the rewards tomorrow," they say. Sadly for some, tomorrow never comes. For others, tomorrow becomes a lonely place because they lost their wife and children along the way.

No one is guaranteed tomorrow. You are the sum of all of your emotions—money cannot satisfy them. Emotions can be satisfied by a contented marriage and happy home and this cannot be purchased with money.

Some form of financial planning for tomorrow is critical but not at the expense of today. Today has its own issues. Don't ignore them because of your greedy plans—you have no guarantee you will have a tomorrow.

If you have fallen in love with money and placed your faith in the almighty dollar, consider the following. The founders of this great nation knew the importance of placing their faith and confidence in God. Look at any U.S. currency, you will find the words, "In God We Trust" printed on it.

The first leaders of the nation wanted future generations to know God is the Source of everything and to remember to place their confidence and trust in Him, rather than in money.

Keep money in its place and health and sufficient wealth will flow to you, rather than from you. Give time and energy to your spouse and children so you will have someone with whom to share your pot of gold when you reach the end of the rainbow. That, my friend, is the real meaning of wealth.

Secret Thirty-One
CHILDREN IN THE MIDDLE

A friend of mine (I will call him Dan) often complained that he and his wife, Sharon, spent too little time together. She was either running the children to a school function, a friend's house, little league practice, or the mall.

Dan had only limited success in pleading with Sharon for more of her time. She claimed her actions benefited the children and that he should be ashamed of himself for trying to divert her attention.

Sharon's obsession with her children was anything but innocent. The truth is, she felt safe when she was immersed in her children's lives. Sharon mistakenly believed if she became too intimate with Dan, he might see her the same way she saw herself. Her poor self-image prevented her from taking the risk.

Sometimes, both spouses lose themselves in their children's lives. Each mutually agrees to neglect the other. Frank and Marge played hide and seek with each other for over twenty-five years. During that time they absorbed themselves in their children's lives and neglected each other.

Though they tried hard, Frank and Marge could not make up for lost time once their kids were grown and gone. Marge left Frank for a man she became intimate with at work.

Matt and Carrie, another couple I'm familiar with, also relied on their children to meet their emotional needs and neglected each other.

Matt endeavored to become little Matthew's best buddy, while Carrie diligently worked at becoming her

133

daughter's girlfriend.

Matt and Carrie also used their children as pawns when they argued. Each would coax a child into taking sides. The kids became both protectors and confidants. Without their children, Matt and Carrie were lost when it came to communicating with each other.

Using children as leverage in an argument is not only manipulative, but a subtle form of abuse. Boys become "mother's little man," or "mamma's big boy." Daughters wear the label of "daddy's girl," or "daddy's little princess." When either spouse plays this fatal game, heartache follows—for them and their children.

However, the saddest relational ploy may be the one involving couples who place the blame for their marital problems on their children. Blaming often sounds like this: "If we would have never had kids, we might still be together." Or, "If my husband could have stood the pressures of raising a family, he might not have left me."

Don't fool yourself. Children don't ruin marriages. Adults do. If your children are causing stress at home then you are probably not acting like a responsible parent. You may need to seek professional help to identify the real cause of your marital problems and assist you in developing a healthier attitude toward your children.

Blaming children is a cowardly way of handling domestic issues. Be a responsible spouse and parent. Place the blame where it belongs, with you and your spouse. Then take immediate steps to save your marriage.

If you are serious about changing your relationship with your spouse, let him or her in on the real problem—your fear of intimacy. Promise to work on your fear together. If professional help is needed, get it. Become a responsible parent. Do it not only for your spouse and children—do it for you.

Secret Thirty-Two
LOVERS' LEAP

When I was a teenager, my friends and I frequented a spot on the outskirts of town affectionately known as "Lovers' Leap." The romantic folklore that fueled its popularity was fascinating to me.

Years later, while working with divorce recovery groups, I discovered similarities between the stories told by the group participants and the romantic tales that stirred my adolescent interest. The group participants had jumped into marriage without examining their motives or weighing the consequences of their actions. Their stories were every bit as tragic as the tale of two lovers leaping to their deaths.

What motivated them to rush into marriage? Some explained how they married their spouse because their friends were getting married and they didn't want to feel left out. Several said they married to escape poverty. Boredom was also a reason for getting married. Others revealed they leaped into marriage to escape loneliness. A few admitted they married the first person that came along to flee repressive parents or an abusive home. Many of them married the first person to propose because they were afraid no one else would want to marry them.

Obviously, most of those who find their way into a divorce recovery program married for all the wrong reasons. However, another revealing fact surfaced in the stories I heard. The majority of participants in the divorce recovery groups I've attended said they married their spouses even though they knew deep down that something wasn't right. In spite of all the warning signs they leaped without thinking about what they were getting themselves into. Moreover, they leaped in spite of the warnings sounded by friends and family. They leaped believing they could fix their spouse or he or she would someday change.

Nothing is romantic or sentimental in the tragic story of two lovers leaping into a relationship or marriage doomed for failure. It will take years to heal the wounds —some never heal. They endure the scars. Ask those who have participated in divorce recovery groups. I'm sure they will agree.

"Must every lover's leap result in heartache and ruin?" you ask. No. It happens only if the couple fails to take a long, hard look at the future of the relationship, refuse to listen to friends or trusted advisors, and ignore the warning sounded by their instincts.

Every marriage requires a leap of faith. To some, faith means acting without first considering all the possible outcomes, or blindly trusting in another without knowing whom they are and what makes them tick. This isn't the definition of faith; it is the definition of foolishness.

Between faith and foolishness is a fine line. I have outlined some tips to help you discern the difference.

▸ First, faith is never groundless. Anyone who professes faith should understand what it is he or she believes in. A person should be able to verbalize his or her faith and explain why they believe as they do.

▸ Secondly, you should also feel an inner calm and a sense of peace about your decision without being fooled into thinking the other person or circumstances will change with marriage or time. Confidence accompanies every well thought-out decision and faith is the quality of a confident individual.

▸ Trust is the third important component of faith. "Trust in whom or in what?" you may ask. Trust involves three areas when it comes to relationships. You must first trust your decision, then you must trust yourself, and finally, you must trust the other person. When love comes calling, check your confidence level. Look within to find a sense of peace and measure your level of trust. If your decision passes this simple test, then no matter what your family and friends may think or say, you can make the right decision and your faith will see you through.

I'm reminded of a friend who nearly went into a state of shock upon hearing that his "baby" sister planned to marry a man ten years her senior. (His baby sister was twenty-four years old at the time, but never mind that.) My friend rushed to her apartment. He screamed, yelled, wept, and groveled in an attempt to dissuade his sister from marrying an older man. His sister and her fiance were disgusted with his behavior, but listened patiently while big brother ranted and raved into the night.

Finally, after hours of intense persuasion, exhaustion and discouragement overtook my friend and he left his sister to her own discretion.

Today my friend laughs when he tells the story of how his baby sister married the most wonderful man in the world. They have been married over fifteen years, have a successful business, three beautiful children and happiness any couple would envy. As my friend likes to say, "It goes to show you that when two people are confident with their decision, at peace with themselves and trust each other, their marriage will work—no matter what others may say."

What about you? Did you leap into love with the faith and feeling that everything would work out well? Or did you jump into marriage or into a relationship without first weighing the magnitude of your decision?

Were you living with someone you knew wasn't right for you, but married them anyway? Are you in the kind of relationship or marriage you wish you had never entered? Are you living with someone who refuses to change? Are you of the opinion that marriage has made no difference and you've given up hope? What can you do?

I can give you several suggestions that others have used to avert disaster after leaping into a relationship or marriage without considering the consequences of their decision. However, I must honestly tell you there are no sure-fire answers.

What I'm about to relate worked for them. Despite whether or not these suggestions produce the results you want, they will at least give you a course of action to follow. If you follow it, you will find the self-confidence and self-esteem you will need to take your life back into your own hands and do what you need to do for you.

You will feel empowered enough to make choices—a feeling you probably haven't felt in some time. If you are ready to become the master of your fate, listen up.

1. My first suggestion is find help. Church groups and self help groups can offer much needed support. They can probably point you to a resource that will enable you to build your self-worth and self-confidence.

   Look in the phone book to find the telephone numbers for the support group right for you.

2. Seek professional guidance. A professional therapist or counselor may be necessary to supplement the assistance you receive from a support group.

   Trained clergy, psychologists or psychiatrists can help you find and use your personal power. Avail yourself of their expertise. Recognize when you can't make it back up the mountain alone. The way may be too uncertain and the climb too steep.

3. If you are religious, ask God to guide you to the right people. Ask Him to give you the insight, courage and strength to do what you need to do when you reach the mountain top again.

Although you may have leaped into marriage and ended up where you don't want to be, you can find recovery if you will follow these few suggestions. It will be difficult. The effort must be great. But so are the rewards.

138

Secret Thirty-Three
ADDICTIONS

Addictions are a major cause of marital and relational problems in America today. Addictions include alcohol, drugs, gambling, sex, shopping, eating, not eating, smoking, pornography, religion, and ad infinitum.

Addictions are ways and means used to escape yourself and gain a sense of equilibrium or empowerment in an otherwise hectic or powerless situation.

People addicted to some activity or substance are tormented by negativity—they feel like victims. They are convinced that others are responsible for their problems and they are powerless to defend themselves or reverse their circumstances. They often indulge in a one-person pity party. They shun responsibility for their life and for the predicament they are in by escaping into obsessive, compulsive behavior again.

People who are dependent on an addiction are also filled with anger and blame others for their problems. The addiction provides temporary relief from soul strangling resentments.

When the temporary soothing effects of the addiction wear off, the addict experiences a profound sense of remorse. The remorse promotes more self-pity and an attitude of, "What's the use." This mind set grants them permission to escape into their addiction again. The addicted person feels as if they are stuck on a merry-go-round and can't get off.

Someone actively engaged in obsessive, compulsive behavior has a life that goes full circle again and again. Today they are practicing abstinence. They experience a reprieve from the destructive effects of the addiction cycle. Then, without warning, the addiction returns and the cycle begins anew.

Jill lived with an alcoholic who drank heavily on weekends. She said there were times when he would stop for a drink Friday after work and not come home until Sunday morning.

On other occasions, he would pick up several cases of beer on the way home from work Friday evening and drink until Sunday night. Monday would roll around, followed by four and half more days of abstinence and another drunken weekend.

Jill tried numerous ploys to save her marriage. She ignored her husband, hoping she could accept his drinking if she immersed herself in other activities. Sometimes she even drank with him, hoping to prove to him that if she could stop he should be able to stop, too.

When these approaches failed, she scheduled counseling sessions. He went to them at first, but gradually began missing appointments, then eventually stopped. Next she tried religious arguments, but they also failed to work.

Jill lived with her alcoholic husband for ten years before she realized her husband's addiction was impossible to deal with on her own. She decided to divorce him.

Addictions defy logic. They defy threats, coercion and advice from well-meaning friends and loved ones. Addictions are cunning, baffling, and powerful. They are too ingrained for the addicted person to kick on their own and too much for their spouse or loved one to deal with.

Addictions cause irreparable damage to relationships and marriages, yet they may be only vaguely recognizable to the innocent bystander.

I know people who stay permanently medicated with prescription drugs so they won't have to face reality. I know others who are addicted to food—they eat to numb their emotional pain.

Then there are those who refuse to eat, hoping to starve their feelings of inferiority. Some are addicted to shopping and other compulsions. Any addiction can be devastating to a relationship or marriage.

How about you? Are you addicted to alcohol, drugs, sex, gambling, shopping, food or some other substance or compulsive behavior? If you are, then you are out of touch with your feelings, alienated from your loved ones and denying reality. Your life is probably characterized by deceit, mistrust, negative thinking and destructive behavior. These negative manifestations are preventing you from experiencing intimacy with your spouse while feelings of remorse are keeping you chained to your addiction.

Are you sick and tired of your obsessive, compulsive behavior? Are you fed up with what it's doing to you, your marriage or relationship? Do you want to stop the destructive cycle? Are you beaten? Are you so defeated you will do anything to gain release?

The same questions apply to any spouse who lives with an obsessive, compulsive person.

If you are sick of the way you are living, listen up—it's nearly impossible to recover on your own. You need help. Your will power alone and best thinking got you where you are.

Here is a list of support groups that can help. Review it and find the program of recovery right for you.

▸ Alcoholics Anonymous offers experience, strength and hope to all who have a desire to stop drinkin~
▸ Alanon is a program designed for those who ~~t and an alcoholic.
▸ Co-Dependents Anonymous i~ program where many find m~ understanding.

Note: Alanon and Co-Dependents Anonymous will help you separate your feelings and needs from those of your spouse or loved one.

- Sexaholics, and Sex and Love Addicts Anonymous are two programs offering help to those who are addicted to love and sex.
- Emotions Anonymous offers wonderful support, too. It will teach you how to manage your feelings rather than allowing your feelings to manage you.
- You may find Relationships Anonymous helpful, particularly if you are dependent upon a relationship or a person for your self-esteem and emotional security.
- Seek professional help. A trained therapist or counselor may be necessary to supplement the assistance you receive from a support group. Avail yourself of their expertise.

Look in the phone book to find the telephone numbers for the support group right for you and your problem. Make the call that will save your life and your marriage. Beat the addiction that is beating on you.

relationship to another trying to satisfy her thirsting soul.

How about you? Do you carry feelings of guilt, shame and inferiority over and over again to the "relationship well," hoping this time you will find the person who will satisfy an empty feeling within?

Is your opinion of yourself based on something someone said or did to you in the past? Does your self-image hinge on the notion that God isn't interested in you and you aren't worthy or deserving of Him or His love? If so you may be going to the relationship well only to draw temporary relief.

The truth that vanquished the Samaritan's feelings of inferiority, eradicated her faulty beliefs, and freed her from the relationship well is applicable to you, too. Finding love's living water can be your greatest breakthrough.

What is this living water? It is knowing the truth about yourself—you are good enough to have everything everyone else has. You have always been worthy of the best life has to offer, but something in your past made you think otherwise. Hence, your dependency on the relationship well.

Where can you find love's living water in the day and age we live in? Many find it in the safety of a 12-Step program. There they feel free to share their pain with others in recovery—others who will love them in spite of what may have happened in the past.

Some find unconditional love and acceptance in their therapist or counselor. Others find it in church or other support group. A lucky few find it in the company of nurturing friends. Some even find it in books such as this one.

Once you have tasted love's living water, you will discover the truth about yourself. You are okay and always have been okay but your abusive past made you think otherwise.

Experience love's living water for yourself, break your

Part Three

The Patient Practice of Love and Marriage

Secret Thirty-Five
LOVE'S STAYING POWER

Erroneous ideas lead to inappropriate behavior. These behaviors often produce difficulties that seem impossible to overcome. If one party in a relationship or marriage can't or won't identify and deal with their personal demons, divorce or separation often results.

Looking back at the issues involved, one may mistakenly presume a lasting relationship or successful marriage is too improbable to achieve and give up hope. In spite of love's painful problems, I discovered what millions of people already know—true love has staying power.

What is the "mystical power" that bonds some relationships and marriages together yet is obviously missing in others? No magic—the bond is created by couples sincerely willing to work at identifying and correcting the root cause of their marital and relationship problems. Love lasts when a couple identifies and works to resolve their character defects rather than hiding them behind a perfectionistic mask or phony facade. Take a personal inventory now and then. It is the secret to love's staying power.

There is a catch. How can you accurately identify a bona fide attempt at self-assessment and self-improvement from one that is counterfeit or void of sincerity?

Some people in the examples in the previous section were unwilling to take inventory of themselves, identify problems, and work at change. They were destined to repeat their mistakes and experience the pain and suffering again and again. Worst of all, by hoping for a different outcome without changing their irrational thoughts and behavior, they hope in vain.

A faulty belief system traps you in a self-defeating

pattern of behavior. Until dysfunctional beliefs are discovered and discarded, nothing will ever be different. An old saying says it all—"If nothing changes, then nothing changes."

Another issue you must consider—do you have what it takes to stand by your spouse or loved one while they work at change? Take the following inventory to determine whether you have the commitment.

1. How well do you know your spouse? How serious is the problem? Do you know? Are you convinced he or she is sincerely trying to stop their destructive behavior and correct their unworkable beliefs?

2. How well do you know yourself? Do you have the fortitude to stick by your spouse while they work at change? Can you provide your spouse unconditional support as patience, love and encouragement while they work on their issues? Do you have the inner strength to persevere?

3. Are you guilty of clinging to the mistaken notion that you can somehow change or "fix" your spouse? Or do you think he or she can change on their own?

Many persons who participate in divorce recovery programs hold on to the false hope that their estranged spouse will someday change. The estranged party may make overtures to their ex-spouse that are interpreted to mean change is desirable, or at least possible. Unfortunately, most people who participate in a divorce recovery group are unable to distinguish fact from fiction when it comes to their lately beloved. They subject themselves to the heartache and disappointment associated with foolish thinking.

To date, I know of no person in any support group with which I have been associated who successfully reclaimed their marriage. Staying power requires *two* willing participants. This brings us to the second, and final set of questions.

1. Are you and your spouse willing to work at improving your marriage?
2. Can you be honest with yourself and each other about your desire to change?
3. Will you work on your own issues rather than try to work on those of your spouse?

If the participants in my divorce recovery groups had married spouses honestly willing to work on their issues, the results could have been different. However, that means both parties would have chosen to stay together. Marriages irretrievably fail because someone wants to leave rather than stay and work things out.

True, authentic love has staying power. Remember the promise, "in sickness and in health, till death do us part?" Stay together, face your problems, and work them out along the way.

Love that stays requires two willing parties. Love that stays needs plenty of patience and encouragement. Love that stays demands hard work. A love that stays to solve marriage's inevitable problems is what *true* love is all about.

Secret Thirty-Six
HOW TO FIND THE LOVE YOU WANT

Millions of people are searching for the perfect relationship. Many consult therapists trying to improve their marriage. Is love impossible to attain?

Despite an earnest desire, relatively few find a satisfactory marriage or relationship. The problem is that people think they are looking for what they call "love" when in reality they can't define what it is they want.

For example, can you describe the kind of relationship you want? Can you describe the type of person to whom you would like to be married or in love with? More pointedly, can you describe the kind of partner or spouse *you* plan to be to the person who falls in love with you?

Without really knowing what you want from a relationship, a spouse, or yourself, you are like a traveler without maps—clueless about how to get to your destination. As a result, you may have marital and relational problems of which you never dreamed.

It took two divorces and several other failed relationships before I finally understood the importance of defining what I wanted before trying to find it. I think you will grasp the truth of this important secret as I share with you how I met my wife, Julia.

Frustrated at the prospect of searching in vain for a satisfying relationship, I decided to sit down and visualize the kind of woman I wanted. I imagined her having blond hair, blue eyes, a sense of humor, and a pleasing personality.

Next, I dreamed of the relationship we would have and the lifestyle we would live. It was all there—two children, a house, two cars, and a dog.

I must admit, I had my doubts. Where in the world would I find someone who would take a chance on me? And what good would it do to find someone if I couldn't keep them?

The negative side of my persona said, "What's the use? You haven't got a chance. Don't get close to someone only to lose them to someone else later. Why subject yourself to more rejection?"

In spite of these self-defeating messages, I was tired of being alone and determined to hold onto my dream. So I took the time to think about what I wanted from myself. The net result was a vigorous self-improvement program, including facing the problems related to my consumption of alcohol and improving my health with diet and exercise.

Next, I decided to narrow the scope of my search for the girl of my dreams. This search phase of my strategy called for frequent visits to museums, theaters, art galleries and church. These were places I envisioned myself finding the girl of my dreams.

As it happened, I never made it to any of them except church. Not settling on just *any* church, I found one large enough to hold plenty of prospects.

I remember well that fateful Sunday morning. I slipped in late, sat near the back and surveyed the congregation. Low and behold, there in the pew in front of me sat the girl of my dreams. To my astonishment she looked precisely as I had imagined.

Shy and smarting from feelings of inferiority, I left church at the close of service without approaching my dream girl. As I drove out of the church parking lot, I resolutely vowed that next Sunday would be different. I would speak to Dream Girl and make my fantasy come true.

The next Sunday found me back in church. I had been thinking of my dream girl all week. I couldn't wait to find her in the congregation. To my delight, she was sitting in the next pew.

As the service drew to a close and we stood for the benediction, Dream Girl looked my way. We seemed magically drawn to each other. Before I knew it, she turned, said "Hello," and introduced herself. I was elated.

Maybe it was false courage or sheer willpower, but something allowed me to secure my dream girl's phone number. My plan was working!

I called her that afternoon. She was home and we exchanged pleasantries. She seemed receptive. Best of all, she was willing to go out with me the very next weekend.

Dream Girl and I went to a swank restaurant for our first date. Afterwards we drove to my house. There, in the seclusion of my home, both of us should have been nominated for an academy award. The master illusionist known as infatuation carried the night. We found in each other what we thought we were looking for—Prince Charming and Cinderella.

Four months after our first date we were engaged. Plans were made for a spring wedding. All was going well. My self-improvement program was working like a charm. It seemed too good to be true. Unfortunately, it was.

I learned that the girl of my dreams was raised in a dysfunctional family. Her father was a practicing alcoholic. Her mother was a member of Al-Anon (a support group for relatives and friends of the alcoholic). Dream Girl had recognized something familiar in me.

Then without warning, I gave Dream Girl cause for concern. I failed to come home after a drunken weekend with the boys. She told her mother and her mother persuaded her to cancel our engagement. Our relationship was over.

What happened to my plan? Where did I go wrong? The answers were obvious. My plan failed because I couldn't stay away from alcohol on will power alone. I could not guarantee that my plan would work.

I was devastated. I felt a profound sense of hopelessness. I felt Dream Girl represented my last chance at marriage. In desperation, I looked for help.

Instead of searching for someone to take the place of the girl of my dreams, I followed the path of a friend who found sobriety in a 12-Step recovery program a year earlier. My life began to change.

Not long after opting for recovery, I met Julia, a blond haired, blue eyed girl who has surpassed all of my former dreams. We dated for a year and then mutually agreed to a fall wedding. Four years later we are blessed with two beautiful daughters.

How did I find my real dream girl? First I decided what I truly wanted and made plans to get it.

Reviewing my past, I now realize that although my plan didn't succeed with Dream Girl, it was the last ounce of pain I needed to motivate me to seek help and change my life for good. Best of all, my real dream girl, Julia, was waiting in the wings.

I believe God stepped in, helped me restructure my imperfect plan so it worked to perfection. Nevertheless, without my determination to change, He would not have helped me. I might have gone through yet another failed marriage.

How about you? Do you know what you want? Have you developed a plan? Are you working it? Or is your marriage or relationship in shambles because you don't know what you really want in a spouse or lover?

Decide what you want out of marriage, a relationship, your spouse and yourself. Write it down along with the steps you need to take to make it work. Then work it.

Secret Thirty-Seven
HOW TO KEEP LOVE

Rick frequently admitted to his wife his fear that she would stop loving him one day and leave him. He often asked her, "Do you love me? Are you sure you love me? There isn't anyone else, is there? You're not going to leave me are you?"

Naturally, Rick's wife was upset by his remarks. She interpreted his suspicion as a lack of confidence in her and in their marriage.

Millions of people share Rick's fear. The dread of losing the love of another is one of the worst fears one can experience. The reasons seem clear.

Most of you have lost the love of another at least once in your lifetime, and once is enough for the jilted veterans of love's fickle game. Afterward, many of your thoughts and actions were meant to prevent this immobilizing wound from recurring.

The loss of love usually occurs when a lover or spouse goes their separate way leaving you feeling rejected and alone. You can also lose the love of another in a second way which can be just as devastating to your emotional well-being. It's the basic loss of love experienced as rejection or abandonment during childhood when the culprit was a parent, relative or other trusted care giver. The loss of a friend or sibling to death, or the loss of a parent through divorce are all experiences that feel like abandonment and rejection.

Whether love abandoned you during childhood or later in life the memory lingers on and, while the pain may have dissipated, the scars remain. These scars explain why you may find it difficult, if not impossible, to believe anyone could truly love you. Your disbelief can become so strong can lead to self-fulfilling behavior.

The loss of love experienced in childhood or even later in life is the genesis of a phobia known as hypervigilance. The person with this phobia develops a set of extra-sensitive, internal sensors. These sensors pick up signals to warn the hypervigilant person of the slightest possibility of rejection.

Corey fit this category. He had been married but lost his wife to another man. Corey never quite recovered. Although remarried for several years, he assumed his new wife would someday leave him too.

Instinctively, Corey had his antenna up hoping to intercept rejection vibes given off by his wife's body language, speech, voice inflection, facial expressions and behavior. Corey's wife had no plans to leave him but she was increasingly unhappy with his behavior so she confronted Corey. He confessed he was afraid of losing her.

With his second marriage teetering on the brink of divorce, Corey sought counseling. During his sessions with the counselor, he discovered the source of his hypervigilance.

A love lost during childhood or later in life can have other devastating effects as well. One effect is to turn the jilted party into a controller. Hoping to avoid further rejection, the domineering person tries to control their spouse or partner's opinions, attitudes, thoughts and behavior.

Nick was a controller. His parents divorced when he was 12-years old and he, as many children do, felt responsible. When Nick became an adult, he vowed no one would ever leave him again. Of course, that meant trouble for any woman who married him.

Nick eventually married. The application of his control tactics soon became so intense that he refused to allow his

157

wife to go anywhere without him. He even told her how to dress and listened in on her phone conversations.

Nick's wife finally had enough. She fled to the arms of an understanding friend. Shortly thereafter, she filed for divorce.

The psychological effects of a love once lost may not stop when the relationship or marriages ends, however. Another phenomenon can occur after one loses at love. The abandoned party often becomes self-absorbed to the point they are unable to focus on the many possibilities for giving love.

The self-absorbed person has only one thing on their mind—protection of their well-being. Self-centered fear fueled by past events still fresh on the victim's mind, burrows itself deep into their subconscious and breeds trouble throughout their life.

When in relationships, the subconscious, self-centered fear sets off a chain reaction in the mind and emotions thus contributing to the very outcome they fear the most. Is it any wonder millions of people are asking the question, "How can I keep love?"

Fortunately, the answer to this perplexing question is practical and easy to understand—you can keep love as long as you give love.

Certainly, as exceptions to the rule, some people gamble with love and win. However, the stakes are high and those who appear to be winning only win for a season.

If giving love is the secret to keeping love, then why don't more people apply this simple truth in their relationships? I believe their history of lost love causes the fear that if they give love they might be rejected. The result is that they simply choose not to give love at all.

Giving love when unpleasant memories remain indelibly stamped on one's mind and emotions is not easy. Courage, a willingness to change, and faith are required to give love when the fear of rejection seems stronger than you are.

A vital step in the process involves forgiving those you feel betrayed you in the past. Forgiveness is the only way to get rid of the nagging memories that block your efforts at expressing love. Refusing to forgive perpetuates painful memories with their corresponding feelings of fear and self-defeating behavior. Forgiveness is absolutely necessary. Without it, you will forever remain hardened in your emotions, hypervigilant in your thinking and self-centered in your actions.

How can you give love when all you have ever concerned yourself with is the prospect of losing love? First of all, giving is more than an action, it's an attitude, too. An attitude of giving is the antithesis of self-centered behavior.

If you are self-centered, here is a practical way to cultivate a giving attitude. As you go through the day think of your spouse first and yourself second. Practice placing his or her interests before your own. Even if you don't feel like it or don't really want to, do it anyway. "Act" as if you want to place your spouse first. Keep "acting as if" until an attitude of giving becomes second nature. Keep giving until your self-centered nature is pushed aside in favor of the brand new you.

Give love and you create a self-perpetuating cycle. One guaranteed to chase away the fear of losing love because you are too busy unselfishly giving love.

Giving love is the only sure means of receiving it. Isn't that the secret you've been looking for?

Secret Thirty-Eight
LOVE IS LIBERATING

An old adage says, "If you let love go and it comes back to you, it was yours all along."

The truth contained in this simple saying is profound, yet frightening. If you seriously consider it, you will quickly realize this wise proverb advocates mentally freeing your loved one and giving them unrestricted freedom to stay or leave. The choice is theirs, not yours.

The stakes are high. However, there are those who know no fear. They seem confident; their relationship has something extra. Faith is the distinguishing characteristic that sets them apart from the fainthearted.

The vulnerable person feels a need to suppress feelings of insecurity. They question their relationship, allowing fear to guide their actions. They try to possess the object of their affection.

The idea of "giving" their loved one the freedom to stay or leave and to think for themselves is a frightening concept for the faint of heart. Manipulation and control become their main objectives. The erroneous idea can be stated this way: "If I can make him or her stay, I'll be happy, and if I'm happy I know I can make him or her happy, too."

Realistically, it is almost impossible to keep someone in a relationship if they want to leave. However, unwilling to let their spouse go, the insecure partner may revert to battering, stalking, intimidation, threats, or emotional abuse.

Warning! Love is never really yours if you have to hold it by force. True love is emancipating. Authentic love says, "Leave if you wish. I love you enough to set you free

160

to do what's best for you, even though I'm not convinced it's best for me."

Thinking you can control another person is sheer folly. Trying to control someone else will result in rebellion and heartache, not loyalty and devotion. Although you may think the person you are trying to control belongs to you, their mind and emotions are somewhere else. Their heart isn't in the relationship and so neither are they. All you have is a reluctant body, a physical presence.

Release the one you love and let them go. When you do, what transpires will seem magical. You will suddenly experience an air of confidence. Your new found sense of surety and poise will make you positively irresistible. The transformation from a fearful and uncertain individual to one who is strong and self-assured can be absolutely captivating.

"Captivating?" you ask. Yes, captivating. The mental release of your loved one gives you an aura of faith and trust that is nothing short of seductive. You will transmit a powerful subliminal message that will impress him or her more profoundly than any efforts at control. Before you know it, they commit to you because they want to.

I realize this concept defies logic and opposes all of our natural instincts. Clearly it runs counter to popular opinion. Yet to miss this secret is to invite disaster into your marriage or relationship.

Personally, I know that love is liberating, not controlling. This secret eluded me for most of my life. I made the mistake of trying to hold my wife prisoner. In fact, all of my past relationships personified the unflattering experience of wearing a "ball and chain." I was the ball, and the other person felt as if they were tethered to an emotional chain.

I held my relationships together by will power alone. All of them were devoid of intimacy, companionship and love. I only fooled myself, however. The other person wasn't really participating. Their minds and spirits were out of my control.

My approach to love has been radically different with my present wife, Julia. I have never tried to hold her against her will or attempt to control her. I learned from my past mistakes that trying to possess the other person doesn't work. What does work? Freedom!

You may ask, "What if I exhibit this courage you speak of and set my loved one free and she leaves me anyway?" The answer is simple. She was never yours in the first place.

I hear many participants in divorce recovery groups explain how their estranged spouse tried to dominate them. They sapped them of their enthusiasm and all that remained was an emotional void that felt like a hole in the pit of their stomach. Most described the departed spouse as a paranoid person who wanted to control their thoughts and actions. None wanted to live with that kind of person any longer.

A major cause of unsuccessful marriages may be this issue of domination and control. The spouse that terminated the relationship wouldn't accept dictatorial rule any longer. He or she absconded with as many material possessions as they could carry, determined never to live as a hostage again. The oppressed spouse had finally summoned the courage to escape the oppressor.

Release your loved one and set them free if you hope to have an enduring relationship or marriage. Experience the joy that comes from knowing that both of you are forever pardoned from serving each others' unreasonable demands.

Begin today to enjoy the many wonderful benefits that come from new found strength, confidence and freedom. Remember the secret. Liberate the person you love so you both become truly free to love without restraint.

Secret Thirty-Nine
LOVE ACCEPTS IMPERFECTION

Commercials show women who are tall, thin and "drop dead" gorgeous. Similar adds depict men as muscular, impeccably well groomed and extremely handsome. This leads some of our present generation to search for someone who doesn't exist. Unfortunately, the advertising industry has brainwashed people to believe otherwise.

The unrealistic images fostered by Madison Avenue are bad enough but another level of intolerance is thriving in today's society. I'm not speaking of the kind of intolerant spirit you can see on a busy street or crowded highway any day of the week, I'm referring to the intolerant attitude spouses exhibit toward each other. Unfortunately, it is an attitude their children take with them into adulthood. In turn, they perpetuate the same level of intolerance in their own marriages and relationships.

Kathy, a friend of mine, complained that her husband seldom had anything nice to say about her.

"He was so critical. I could never please him. Nothing I did was good enough. I could never say or do the right thing. My dresses were either too tight or too loose. One day he would accuse me of flaunting my attributes and the next day of being a prude. He even found fault with my hair. It was either too short or too long. He *always* found something to criticize. I wonder if he even loved me?" she asked.

The answer is not simple. The problem wasn't Kathy's inability to do things right; the problem was her husband's unwillingness to take responsibility for himself and his own happiness. Kathy's husband felt powerless and he punished her for the way he felt.

A second reason Kathy's husband seemed obsessed with pointing out her faults was that he was intensely afraid of intimacy. He used criticism to fend off any accidental or unwanted intrusion into his innermost life. As a result, Kathy stayed busy trying to correct her shortcomings and avoid further criticism while her husband stayed within himself.

Kathy had issues too. She suffered from the irrational idea of perfectionism. The idea, "If I'm the perfect wife (or husband), my spouse will be pleased with me and he won't have an excuse to leave me." Or, "If I do everything precisely the way he wants things done, he is sure to love me."

The person with this false belief assumes that if they attain perfection their spouse won't have a legitimate reason to leave them. Consistently meeting another person's expectations will make them too valuable to abandon. The fear of rejection and abandonment locks its prey tightly in the perfection trap.

Many problems are associated with perfectionistic behavior. First, perfection is unattainable for humans. As a result, the guarding and pretense to try to sustain the illusion of perfection makes intimacy impossible.

Secondly, perfectionism is fueled by fear, not love. True love doesn't set unrealistic standards or deal in unfair criticism.

Thirdly, trying to live the lie of perfectionism places a person under constant pressure to maintain a role. Performing a role requires constant vigilance and becomes exhausting. Sooner or later the real you will appear.

Kathy finally realized that what she and her husband had together wasn't love. Their relationship was based on mutual dependency and unrelenting fear which translated into criticism and perfectionistic behavior.

Kathy eventually filed for divorce and enrolled in a divorce recovery program. With the help of her support group she discovered that true love accepts imperfection.

If you want to know whether your relationship is truly founded on love or on emotional dependency, ask yourself these simple questions:

- What is the source of my self-esteem?
- Does my self-esteem come from personal strength or am I depending on my spouse to make me feel good about myself?
- Why am I overly critical of him or her?
- Is it because I'm afraid of intimacy?
- Am I trying to attain perfection, hoping that my wife or husband won't have a legitimate reason to leave me and will love me more?

Whether you are guilty of living the perfectionistic lie or are the one who has been unreasonably critical, here's the secret to finding the help you need.

First, realize you won't find happiness or approval by seeking it outside yourself. A negative attitude and self-defeating behavior are road blocks keeping you from experiencing this beautiful secret for yourself. Drop the unrealistic standard you've set for yourself or that someone else has set for you. Accept your imperfect humanity.

If you are the one guilty of unfair criticism by demanding your spouse or loved one meet your unrealistic expectations, ask their forgiveness and take responsibility for your own happiness.

If Kathy and her husband had understood this secret they could have loved each other, imperfections and all. Their self-confidence, self-esteem and ultimate happiness would have come from within and not from another person.

How about you? Are you depending on your spouse or someone else for happiness and approval? If you are, this secret can save your marriage and your relationship. Discover how building your self-esteem and self-confidence can lead to contentment.

Secret Forty
LOVE OFFERS FORGIVENESS

Love and forgiveness are one and the same. In fact, we love through the act of forgiveness.

It's easy to love someone who consistently meets our expectations, but to love someone in spite of their actions is love indeed.

The word "tender-hearted" comes from the Greek word *eusplanchnos*. It means tenderly compassionate. It takes a tender-hearted person to offer forgiveness when someone they love hurts or disappoints them.

A story a friend (I will call him Bob) told me illustrates my point. He said that one afternoon his wife opened the mail to see an additional amount of debt of which she was unaware on their Visa bill. When she finished reviewing the statement, she slowly raised her head and looked into his eyes.

Fear shook him and his mind began to race. "Should I tell her the truth? What will she think of me if I do? Maybe I should make something up? What can I tell her?"

Uncomfortable with his choices and with time running out, Bob decided to tell the truth. He spoke quickly, completing his explanation in a minute or two, then waited anxiously for his wife's response. After a moment of reflection she looked at him and replied, "I understand. I forgive you."

At that moment her tenderhearted, compassion drowned his fears in a sea of forgiveness.

Tenderhearted compassion, summarized as forgiveness, drew them closer, when harboring resentment would have driven them apart.

Several weeks later, Bob asked his wife why she forgave him. She told him, "No one's perfect. I used our credit card on occasion, hoping you wouldn't find out." She went on to say that holding him to a standard she couldn't maintain wasn't fair to him or her.

My friend's story contains the essential elements of tenderhearted, compassionate love expressed as forgiveness. First, he admitted his mistake—you can't be forgiven if you refuse to admit you've done something wrong.

People often refuse to acknowledge their mistakes because they falsely assume their spouse wouldn't like them if they knew the truth about them. Ironically, this thought process alienates them from the one who would love them the most if given the opportunity. The opportunity is best when you are at your worst.

When Bob admitted his mistake, his wife forgave him because she had forgiven herself for similar transgressions in the past. This is the second essential element found in heartfelt forgiveness.

When you hold yourself to unrealistic standards, you will hold your spouse to unrealistic standards too. You will find it as difficult to forgive them as you do yourself when you make mistakes.

The inability to forgive is rooted in the unrealistic belief that everyone should behave perfectly all the time. Refusing to forgive yourself or your spouse while trying to hold him or her and yourself to unrealistic standards is tantamount to playing God. If God, Who is perfect, willing forgives when asked, why can't you forgive your spouse or loved one?

The only thing to be gained by refusing to forgive is an illusion of self-righteousness. You are only hurting yourself when you deal in illusions. Furthermore, holding on to resentments will cause serious harm to your emotional and spiritual health. No one ever gained love by refusing to forgive. This is true for you as well as for the one who disappointed you.

Avail yourself of the spirit of forgiveness. After all, forgiveness is a two-way street paved with compassion and traveled only by the tenderhearted.

Secret Forty-One
LOVE IS BLAMELESS

I tried and failed at two previous marriages and other relationships between. Although those experiences were painful, they provide valuable insight into my thought life.

In the past, I thought the best marriages and relationships went to the most handsome and self-assured individuals. Convinced I was lacking in both these qualities, I resorted to acting. I worked hard to make myself appear as youthful, self-confident and successful as possible. The unsuspecting woman in my scenario saw me as a man who was going places. In reality, I knew I was going nowhere.

I could sustain my performance for four or five months. Then I would begin behaving as the person I believed myself to be—flawed and unworthy of a relationship with anyone pleasing and nice. My acute inferiority feelings would provoke me to act inappropriately.

I won't bore you with my past antics. Suffice it to say the person I turned into wasn't the real me either. It was the me imprinted on my subconscious mind in the form of a poor self-image. This image was forced on me by a childhood that included emotional abandonment, stern religiosity, rejection and unsympathetic educators.

What kind of person did my loved one invariably see? I would describe him as a jealous, angry, paranoid individual, bent on proving how undeserving he was of the marriage or relationship he had worked so hard to attain.

Frequent bouts with alcohol, gambling and womanizing were all manifestations of a poor self-image and a deep-seated desire to self-destruct. My low self-esteem and poor self-image controlled my thought life and my actions simply followed suit.

It is not difficult to see why I flunked marriage and relationships in the school of hard knocks. Knowing what I do now about my thinking patterns, it's obvious I set myself up to fail from the start. With that in mind, I have had to reassess whether or not I'm really to blame for my marital and relational problems.

My answer may surprise you, but I concluded that I was not to blame. I can say with a clear conscience that I did the best I could with what I knew at any given point in time. If I could have done better, I would have, but I couldn't.

I'm not blaming anyone else either. I'm aware that some people would have me blame my parents, teachers or even my preacher for the way I behaved, but they did the best they could do too. Like me, if they could have done better, chances are they would have.

Another side of my story wonders at the thinking patterns of the women who married me. What was it about me they found attractive? You know some of my history now and can surmise why I behaved the way I did, but what was going on in their minds that made me seem like a prize catch?

I don't mean to demean anyone, but the women in my life saw something in me that looked familiar. Maybe it was my addictions, fears of intimacy or phony facade. Whatever it was, it must have seemed natural. Each of them took my problems personally and assumed most of the blame for our marital difficulties. Was this a coping skill they learned at home?

They would often ask me, "What is it about *me* that causes you to act this way? Haven't I done all that any woman could possibly do? What can I do to prevent this from happening again? Are you so unhappy with me that you feel you need to behave this way? What am *I* doing that causes you to do and say such horrible things to me?"

One other trait was prevalent in the women who tried to love me. Each thought they could "fix" me. Threats, intimidation, retaliation, interventions, legal tactics, forced counseling and unsolicited advice from well-meaning friends and relatives were some of the strategies my ex-wives used to try to change me.

Sometimes I played along and the relationship appeared to improve for a while. At other times, I rebelled, dug in my heels and steadfastly refused any prescribed remedy. Their fortitude and dogged determination were amazing, yet all of their strength and endurance couldn't outlast my insolence.

The dynamics behind my marital relationships might cause you to assume that my ex-spouses were responsible for our problems. I emphatically state they were not. They too, were doing the best they knew how at the time. If they could have done better they would have, but they couldn't.

I have persuaded you to believe no person is to blame for my past problems. Therefore, you might be tempted to blame the stars, fate, luck or God. Don't. Although life isn't fair at times, I am convinced I needed every painful breakup and hurtful experience in order to find the recovery, hope and happiness I now enjoy.

Life is a journey. All of you are here to learn, improve and grow into the persons you are meant to be. Each of you must find your own path to fulfillment. In spite of what may happen along the way, the destination is still the same—freedom from negative beliefs and unworkable behavior learned early in life.

The behaviors, false beliefs and irrational ideas obstructing you from achieving higher consciousness must be uprooted and eliminated. Think of problems as the tools you can choose to use to shape yourself into the man or woman you want to be.

Don't foolishly blame yourself or others for what happened in the past or for what you are experiencing now.

171

When you play the "blame game" you are saying in effect, "Life isn't fair," and "I'm not responsible for the mess I'm in." When you blame yourself, you are saying, "I'm a louse, and I hate myself for screwing up my life."

Life *isn't* fair and you are not to blame. However, you are responsible. You are responsible for where you are now and for what you are presently experiencing even though your past may have contributed mightily to your circumstances.

Stop blaming yourself or others for what happened in the past. Do take responsibility for where you are today. Review your mistakes. Learn from the past and use the knowledge to do better in the future. You have the power to become the person you were meant to be.

Secret Forty-Two
OWN YOUR FEELINGS

Feelings can cause problems, especially when you allow them to control your behavior.

Jack had trouble with feelings of anger and fear. He would become angry with his wife over something she did and fuss and fume at her for hours. After his anger subsided, fear would take over and Jack worried that his wife might not forgive him for the way he treated her. He would then hibernate in the family room and suppress his feelings with peanuts and beer, only to reenact the same scene the next time his anger got the best of him.

As with many people, Jack failed to realize an important truth about feelings. Feelings are a natural physiological reaction to external stimuli. However, a person does not have to act out in response to them. Nor is it necessary to suppress feelings because of guilt or shame.

Rhonda managed her feelings inappropriately. When she felt angry with her husband and children, she would stuff her feelings until she exploded in a fit of rage, or she would go stay at a relative's house until her temper cooled down. Rhonda wasn't aware that angry feelings are a signal something is wrong.

Thinking you either have to act on your feelings or deny them only causes difficulties. The problems you experience because of what you are feeling stems from the way you mismanage your feelings, not from the feelings themselves.

When Rhonda suppressed her feelings because she felt guilty for having them, she became irritable with her family. She lived in denial by staying busy with household chores or playing personal servant to her children.

Rhonda's husband and children disrespected her because she refused to respect herself by honoring her feelings.

In Jack's case, he expressed his feelings inappropriately and then felt sorry for the way he acted. The feelings of remorse and fear he felt afterwards affected his self-esteem. He was stuck in a cycle he didn't know how to break away from.

Don't deny your feelings; you are inviting disrespect when you do. If your spouse, or anyone else, senses you are ignoring your feelings, they will invariably cross the line. Your ego will fight back in an effort to maintain some sense of dignity. Consequently, it is important to respond appropriately to feelings.

Many people don't know how to handle feelings appropriately because their parents modeled poor coping skills at home. You will do what you remember your parents doing in similar situations unless you make changes in your responses when you are an adult.

Neither Rhonda nor Jack knew how to handle feelings because their role models possessed poor coping skills too.

How should a person handle feelings? Jack could have calmly talked to his wife about what had happened and how it made him feel.

In Rhonda's case, she could have told her family she was going to express how she feels each day. She could ask them to respect her feelings.

There are other techniques a person might use to manage feelings. For example, taking a walk or other exercise can help defuse anger. Sometimes it is wise to withhold a response until the anger subsides. Some people write letters then throw the letters away as a means of venting their anger. I even know a few people who own punching bags.

Regardless of what you choose to do, don't ignore your feelings because your feelings will not ignore you.

Feelings define where you are at any given point in

time. Denying your feelings is to deny the truth about what you are experiencing. Denying your experience is to deny reality.

If you feel a feeling, then own it. It's yours. I don't know how often I walked around with a phony smile plastered on my face when I was seething with anger inside. I can't count the times I pretended to be a strong, immovable rock when all the while I was scared out of my wits.

When I deny my feelings and act like something I'm not, that is called living a lie. Others see through my act and disrespect me for my lack of sincerity. When you feel your feelings you are being genuine—you are being yourself. Genuine people are loved and revered. Impostors are not.

Feelings left unattended, suppressed or misdirected will have negative consequences on your physical, mental, emotional and spiritual well-being. Think about the times you stuffed your feelings or acted them out inappropriately. Did your blood pressure elevate, your muscles tense and your head ache?

Think about the effect your unseemly behavior had on your spouse. Did your actions cause them to back off? Did you feel alienated from the major person in your life?

Can you recall a time when you expressed your feelings constructively? I bet you felt better faster and the painful event passed without the slightest headache or upset stomach. Best of all, your feelings had little or no effect on your marriage or relationship.

What does it mean "to own" your feelings? It means acknowledging them, allowing them to run their course and expressing them in a way that isn't harmful to your relationship or your health.

In short, if you manage your feelings, your feelings won't manage you. Take this advice with you and live by it. You will be glad you did.

Secret Forty-Three
SETTING BOUNDARIES

Imagine a world with no boundaries to clearly define one country from another, or one city, state or county from the other? It would be virtually impossible to maintain a common set of laws and preserve common values, customs and traditions?

Without boundaries there would be no feeling of community and no sense of identity. Without boundaries a country would become a transitory state lacking stability and importance.

Boundaries emphatically declare. "This is my territory." A definite body of rules and ordinances, agreed upon norms, and specific ways of doing things that, when added together, define an entity and what it stands for.

The Revolutionary War slogan, "Don't Tread on Me," united the colonists in the fight for independence. Without this powerful slogan, the United States of America may never have become a reality. On a personal level, without it, your self-respect may never become a reality either.

I believe the famous Revolutionary War slogan should hang in every school room and day care center across our country. It embodies the ideas of reverence and respect for boundaries, whether they are the boundaries of a nation, city, state, or an individual.

Unfortunately, some people don't have the colonists' spirit. They seem to wear a bright neon sign that reads, "Please Tread on Me." They suffer from poor self-esteem and almost no self-confidence. They become Nice Guys, Sweethearts, and People Pleasers to try to win the acceptance and approval of others. They seem to think popular opinion is the true standard for determining their self-worth.

People who seem to have no definite boundaries allow their spouse, friends, family and neighbors to treat them with disrespect. These persons never voice an objection to being treated badly. They are also the people whose passive/ aggressive personalities eventually explode in a volcanic eruption that spews anger and rage far more intensely than the immediate situation warrants.

Boundaries can sometimes become a problem. Some people establish such impenetrable boundaries that no one can get close to them because they are so fearful of attack. These individuals resemble human porcupines with their quills extended to protect them from intruders.

It is easy to discern the boundaries of various countries, states, provinces and cities. Their borders are distinctly marked and their shores clearly posted. Even their air space is plainly defined. It is not as easy for individuals to establish reasonable boundaries.

How close is too close when it comes to measuring the appropriate distance between you and another person? What constitutes acceptable contact? Have you set boundaries to protect your physical well-being? Are they different from those you established to protect your emotional health?

Hopefully, you have established reasonable boundaries, physical and emotional, that allow you to experience intimacy without inviting disrespect.

NOTE: This might be a good time to ask your spouse how he or she would describe your boundaries?

Men typically set a larger circumference of protective defenses than women set because men don't do well with feelings. They prefer to keep their spouse at a distance so they can measure their own responses and guard their emotions.

Women, however, seem less concerned with boundaries. They often maintain too small a circle of protection for their own good. They often seem to wear their feelings on their sleeves and their responses come straight from the heart.

Women may tend to give their husbands free access to their personal space by failing to establish parameters that will protect their physical and emotional dignity.

Penny told her divorce recovery group that although she allowed her husband to do as he pleased, he still wasn't happy. He spent as much time as he wanted with his friends and used pornography for sexual gratification when he didn't feel like being physically intimate with her.

Penny even permitted him to use dope in their home and party with his friends on weekends. Eventually, he began flirting with Penny's girlfriends and invited one of them to spend the night with him. When Penny found out, she was devastated.

"What went wrong?" she demanded.

The answer is simple. Penny mistakenly believed by giving in to her husband, he would be content and wouldn't leave her. The fear of rejection caused Penny to discount her interests and invalidate her feelings. Because of her fear, she allowed her husband to take advantage of her by crossing boundaries of paramount importance to her self-respect and personal dignity.

Tim's experience was much different from Penny's. He told his divorce recovery group that he established broad boundaries in his marriage. He established his boundaries so high and wide that no one could get close, not even his wife.

Tim's weakened self-esteem convinced him that if his wife really knew him, she wouldn't like him. The fear of rejection caused Tim to set boundaries that destroyed his marriage, rather than preserve it.

Most people enrolled in divorce recovery programs

failed to set reasonable boundaries. In my groups, 60 percent of them were women. Their boundaries were so obscure that their ex-spouses were invading their personal space long after the divorce was final.

Sometimes, this invasion continues until the assailed party realizes they are living in an occupied state with their ex-spouse filling the role of conquering dictator.

Many male participants in divorce recovery groups made the same mistake Tim made. They set boundaries preventing their spouse from getting too close and destroyed their marriages in the process.

Where are your boundary lines drawn? Are they so wide no one, not even your spouse, can get close to you? Or have you neglected to set boundaries at all, hoping to appease your spouse or loved one with your compliance?

The history of relationships shows appeasement doesn't work and impenetrable boundaries only serve to separate us from those who would love us if they only had the chance.

You may have to redefine your boundaries if you finally realize they have prevented you from experiencing intimacy and are detrimental to your relationship. It's never too late to reset boundaries or draw new ones.

On the other hand, if you have failed to establish boundaries in your marriage, then draw the lines now so you can reclaim your self-respect and personal dignity. Whether your marriage is a success or failure may depend on how well you do.

Secret Forty-Four
EXPECTATIONS

Beware of expectations. They form the basis for experiencing either happiness or discontentment in a relationship or marriage. Think back to your expectations—past and present.

For example, I'm personally close to a man whose personal expectations were quite high. He married at a young age. He and his equally young bride moved to a large Midwestern city, found an apartment, and bought a car. He enrolled in college. She found a job.

This man fully expected him and his new bride would enjoy physical and emotional intimacy together. He expected her to support him financially while he completed college. He expected her to share his zeal for spiritual things. He expected her to participate with him in his career as a minister. He assumed his wife understood his expectations and she would meet them with no questions asked. He was wrong.

In retrospect, the man must have thought his wife was clairvoyant and could read his mind. Despite his reasoning, the reality is that he failed to communicate his expectations to her both before and after they were married. And she failed to communicate her expectations to him.

Have you caught on? The man I have described is me. I paid dearly for my miscalculation. Disappointment and disillusion began to be my primary emotions. I began to view my wife through critical eyes. I wondered why she seemed reluctant to support my efforts and why she refused to show enthusiasm for my plans.

My wife's expectations were quite different from mine. She expected little things like the rent being paid on time, groceries in the pantry, a reliable car to drive, nice clothes to wear, a savings account and a stable future. Sensing I was either unwilling or unable to meet her expectations, trepidation and fear began to overtake her.

Both of us grew more unhappy and apprehensive with each passing day. We emotionally distanced ourselves from each other. Intimacy was nonexistent in any form and we hardly ever spoke.

We lived this way with the relationship getting progressively worse until I completed college. After graduation we moved back home and pretended that everything was okay. Failing to comprehend the power of unmet expectations, we continued to live in separate worlds and hold each other responsible for our personal dissatisfaction. This went on for five years until my wife finally had enough. She filed for divorce.

Confused and disbelieving, I still didn't understand how unmet expectations had contributed to our problems. It wasn't until much later that my mistake became clear to me. Instead of telling my wife how I felt, I secretly blamed her for our problems and held an incredible grudge. Sadly, I erroneously believed she would someday see how unhappy I was and "wise up." She never did.

Several years later, I realized my wife mistakenly believed that I would come to my senses and see how unhappy she was and "wise up." But I didn't. Failing to communicate our expectations to each other ensured that someday they would come back to haunt us.

Communication is the key ingredient in any successful marriage. I failed to realize that and neglected to share my expectations with my wife. She in turn neglected to share hers with me. Without communication, we acted on erroneous assumptions. Both of us felt discounted and unloved.

Don't take your expectations for granted. They may seem simple to you and easy to understand, but they aren't—unless you talk about them openly. Unspoken expectations can build into a catastrophic problem.

The troubles caused by unmet expectations can be corrected by talking. Make the time to discuss them. If you share your expectations and agree on how you can both meet your own and each others, it will enhance your marriage rather than destroy it.

Secret Forty-Five
GETTING YOUR NEEDS MET

Literally millions of adults have no idea how to go about getting their needs met. As children they were neglected and emotionally abandoned. Many of them enter marriage only to encounter more neglect and emotional abuse.

Unable to stand up for themselves and unskilled at identifying their needs, these ill-fated individuals are often reduced to a subordinate role in all of their adult relationships. Christy fell into this category. She grew up with an alcoholic father and a mother who was a classic enabler.

Christy revealed to her divorce recovery group how her mother seemed obsessed with finding father when he went out on one of his weekly drinking binges. Mother believed it was her duty to make sure Christy's father didn't try to drive home drunk and kill himself or someone else.

Christy spent night after night alone while mother and father played cat and mouse with each other. Even when her parents were home, they wasted their time together by arguing over father's escapades the night before.

When Christy grew older, she accompanied her mother while she searched the nightclubs and taverns for father. By then, he was not only the most important person in mother's world, but in Christy's too.

Christy fell in love with Michael when she turned twenty-one. There was something familiar about him. Michael came from a well-to-do family and his parents took every opportunity to spoil him. From the beginning, Christy instinctively knew her role.

Christy wanted to fulfill Michael's every wish but

after only two years of marriage she realized that something was wrong. Christy wasn't getting any of her own needs met. She grew tired of spending all her time and energy trying to please Michael.

When she confronted him with her own needs, he threw a tantrum and accused her of thinking only of herself. Christy knew then that she was married to a man who would never be able to meet her needs—a man just like her father.

Christy moved in with a girlfriend. Soon she found a therapist. Over the next several months the therapist helped Christy see that unmet needs were the root cause of her marital problems, and how her relationship with Michael was linked to her past.

Christy faced her problem. It wasn't long until she decided to divorce Michael. The decision was sealed when he refused to see the therapist and continued to make unreasonable demands of her.

Steve is another person with unmet needs. His problem was also rooted in negative childhood experiences.

Steve's mother and father were strict disciplinarians who immersed themselves in their careers. When they did manage to find time to spend an evening at home, Steve and his four brothers had to toe the line while his parents read various reports and planned the next day's business.

Steve was the oldest child. This meant he received even less attention than his younger siblings. Steve learned to place his own needs behind those of his brothers. This neglect and subservience would go on until Steve exploded in a fit of rage. He would rant at his parents until they gave him the attention he needed and deserved.

At 19, Steve left home and joined the Army. After his discharge four years later, he moved back to his hometown and took up residence in a tiny apartment. Soon he found work at a local factory and enrolled in night school. At school, he met and subsequently married a woman ten years his senior.

Steve's wife was not only beautiful, she was an aspiring CPA as well. After graduation she landed a job at a large accounting firm and her career took off. In three short years, she received several promotions. Work demanded more and more of her time.

Steve felt a certain affinity for his wife though it perturbed him when she spent long hours at the office. As time went on, Steve's wife was even spending weekends there. Steve felt as if he was living alone.

Steve wasn't sure whether he was loved or not. One thing was certain. His wife was either too busy or too tired to give him the love and attention he needed and wanted.

In spite of how he felt, Steve seemed to have "the patience of Job." He would go along, minding his own business, too afraid to say anything to his wife about his unmet needs until he couldn't stand the neglect any longer.

Without warning, Steve would rant and rave at her, demanding she submit to his need for physical and emotional intimacy and threatening to leave if she refused.

Steve's wife was shocked by his behavior. She had no idea he was so angry. She would immediately grant Steve's wishes, hoping to calm his temper. However, she would ultimately neglect him again until the next time he acted out.

Why couldn't Steve get his needs met as an adult? The same reason most people can't—they don't ask for what they want. It's as if you don't want to inconvenience anyone, especially your spouse.

This sounds, and is, absurd. Nonetheless, many people are ashamed of their needs. They feel guilty for feeling needy. They think it's more honorable to place others before themselves.

Why are you convinced your needs are bad or selfish? It is due in a large part to what happened in your child-

185

hood. The grownups in your life shamed you when you tried to express your needs. You may have been called self-centered, inconsiderate, or greedy when you asked to have your needs met.

Believing the grownups in your life were perfect, you assumed you were at fault for feeling needy. Anymore the term "needy" is viewed as a label which any reasonable person will go to great lengths to avoid, but, everyone is needy at times—it is part of being human. Trying to deny you have needs is futile. Sometimes, people play God by attempting to meet everyone else's needs while discounting their own.

Don't misconstrue what I'm saying. All of you know people who are "bottomless pits," whose needs can't be satisfied no matter how much we do for them. Their needs are obvious to everyone and, in their minds, more important than anyone's.

I'm speaking to the majority of people like you and me who find it difficult, if not impossible, to express their needs.

How about you? Do you feel as if you are giving and never getting? Do you feel as if you are constantly toiling to meet the needs of your spouse and family but no one seems concerned about your needs? A lot of women seem to fall into this category. Men, more often than not, are the culprits when it comes to neglecting the needs of others. Still, there are men, like Steve, who see no other way to get their needs met except by acting out inappropriately.

Most of us learned to devalue our needs as children. Although I realize you had no control over the circumstances in your childhood that prevented you from getting your needs met, today you are an adult and that is no longer the case. You can be in control, at least of yourself. You are responsible for seeing to it that your needs are met.

This is not a license to disregard your spouse's needs

as you take whatever means are necessary to get your needs met, or behave selfishly to the detriment of your family. However, it does mean you should sit down with your wife or husband and explain your needs and how you want to meet them.

Your needs define who you are. If you are suppressing them then you are essentially saying, "I don't want you to know who I am. I'm afraid to tell you for fear you might reject me or dislike me."

If your spouse is ignoring your needs, he or she is saying in effect, "I'm more interested in myself and my needs than I am yours." And, "I really don't care to get to know you; I'm too wrapped up in myself."

Can you see why it's imperative to communicate your needs and take the necessary steps to see they are understood and met? Should you neglect to take these steps, you will have missed an opportunity to get to know each other on an innermost personal level. What a tragedy!

Aim for a warm, intimate relationship established by a mutual desire to understand and meet each other's needs.

Secret Forty-Six
LOVE IS TOUGH

Love bears all things, believes all things, hopes all things, and endures all things. This paraphrase of a verse from the Bible identifies the four rugged characteristics of love. None of them are exclusive from the other.

The couple who bravely bears the problems of life while continuing to believe in each other and hope for a brighter tomorrow will endure the trials and tribulations of today. Their love is tough enough to last.

How about you? Will your love bear all things? Will it stand up under financial hardship, the loss of health, the loss of a loved one, problems with children, in-laws, bosses or friends?

How about fate's fickleness—unfair circumstances swept our way on the unpredictable currents of life?

It's easy to sustain a relationship or marriage when times are good and life is smooth, but what will happen when you encounter turbulent seas?

Will your love withstand the blustery waves of undeserved criticism that sometimes toss us from bow too stern? What about the violent gales where the winds of rejection and abandonment swirl? When can you declare an "all calm" once threatening storm clouds darken an inferiority-riddled personality? Where will you find the strength to bear up under the fierce tempest caused by strained sexual relations? Can you manage your personal and spousal responsibilities while everything around you seems to be going wrong?

These are but a few of the storms that disrupt a person's life from time to time. There are others.

For instance, most couples face daily financial,

physical or emotional problems. Although they may seem minor at first, they can build up to become a serious, destructive force.

Henry's marriage failed partly because of financial strain. His wife couldn't stand the stress of monetary uncertainty any longer. She wanted economic security, while he seemed content to spend their hard-earned money to support his drug habit.

Wayne's wife left him because she refused to continue to support his alcoholism and gambling addiction.

It took a great deal of strength and courage to do what these women did. Staying would have been easy because it was familiar. The strength to leave is one of the ironies of love. Love is tough enough to withstand the turbulent winds of life and tough enough to take wings and fly away.

A tough love doesn't ask you to remain in an abusive or destructive relationship. Staying in a co-dependent, enabling, or otherwise destructive situation is not love.

Is your love tough? Have you been through your share of ups and downs, yet you and your spouse stayed the course until your relationship reached placid seas once more? No doubt you believe in each other.

Believability is the second ingredient found in tough love. A love that is tough only believes the believable. It has no part in manipulation, deceit or denial.

A transitory love, however, is susceptible to believing a lie and clinging to false hope. A case in point—Seth often promised his wife he would stop his affair with a co-worker, straighten out their finances, pay the creditors, save money, repair the leaky faucet and mow the lawn. Remorse, guilt and shame over his sexual and emotional infidelity with the other woman compelled him to make promises he couldn't keep.

Seth's wife wanted to believe him. The sad fact is he proved to be unbelievable.

A tough love is comprised of two creditable people

who believe in each other. They say what they mean and mean what they say. Tough love believes the believable and draws the line between truth and fiction. It is tough enough to face painful truth.

Are you tough enough to accept the truth about your spouse? Can you face the truth about yourself, your relationship or your marriage? If so, then you have reason to hope for a better tomorrow. Don't be confused, however. A love that is tough hopes only when there is reasonable cause to hope.

Are you hoping against hope that your spouse will change? Maybe you think you can fix him? Do you have reason to hope, or are you hoping for the impossible or maybe the improbable? Your answer is important because a relationship is over when all hope is gone. Hope leaves when either spouse is no longer believable.

Plenty of hope is necessary for a marriage to last a lifetime. Hope, belief and the ability to bear up under the storms of life are the prerequisites for endurance. (Endurance is an outward manifestation of an inner strength and fortitude. Some have it; others don't.)

The statistics say 50 percent of marriages fail because of the lack of endurance.

Do you have the endurance to beat the odds? Is your love tough? Will it bear all things? Will it believe all things? Is it filled with hope? If so, then your chances are better than fifty/fifty that your relationship or marriage will endure.

Want higher odds? You and your spouse might reflect on the following: Are you willing to bear the bearable, believe the believable, hope for the achievable and endure the endurable? If you both answered "yes," then you have a love tough enough to last a life time.

Secret Forty-Seven
IT CAME TO PASS

Although the phrase, "and it came to pass," appears 430 times in the Bible, people often ignore it as if it is nothing more than a boring introduction to the story about to unfold. Nevertheless, this phrase puts everything into perspective. Whether it precedes a tale of victory or one of woe, it is an important clue for things to come.

Think back to all the problems you encountered in your lifetime. Think also of all the wonderful blessings that have come your way. All have one thing in common—they came to pass. None came to stay. Whatever you were worried about, last year, last month, or last week is a faint recollection. The achievement or goal you celebrated yesterday is but a flickering memory.

Today, the phrase, "And it came to pass" appears in a somewhat different form, it reads, "This too shall pass." This adaptation was made popular by 12-step programs. They have given this helpful slogan to countless people over the years. It has coaxed millions from the brink of hopelessness and despair and saved many more from making an unwise decision in the face of what seemed to be an unrelenting problem at the time.

When bad things appear, you often find yourself at a crossroads. If you falsely assume the problem is permanent, personal or pervasive, you may do something foolish to harm your marriage or yourself.

If you arrogantly presume that any good fortune you may be experiencing is here to stay, you could unwittingly be setting yourself up for disappointment and heartache later. Nothing is forever. Everything comes to pass.

Consider the following problems that may come your

way from time to time—but fortunately don't come to stay. First, there is the storm of financial difficulty. Experience shows that even feelings of economic insecurity pass. The next paycheck can make last month's bills an old worry.

More serious is the sudden loss of a job and the problems associated with unemployment. All of us know people who have been displaced from their jobs because of corporate mergers and downsizing. A majority of them eventually found jobs for which they were better suited. Their problems didn't stay. They passed.

You may experience the heartache caused by a disobedient child. Everyone was once a child who evolved through phases of unacceptable behavior. As you grew and matured, the inappropriate behavior seen in developmental phases passed.

Illnesses, family squabbles, and feelings of guilt and remorse over wrongs, real and imagined, also pass.

New problems are always on the horizon. Old ones are barely visible in the distance. That's life.

Good times and good fortune also come to pass but may bring human discontent with them. For example, you delight in a promotion only to feel discontented once the thrill wears off and you face new and additional responsibilities.

How about the shiny, new car that gives you a warm feeling, or the bigger house in the better neighborhood that gives delight—until you begin making the payments.

Balance in life is achieved when you refuse to ride an emotional roller coaster, obsessing over a problem one minute and being exhilarated over a temporary accomplishment the next.

Relish the successes and grieve the losses, but wear good fortune and bad like a loose fitting garment. Remember. Everything comes to pass; nothing comes to stay.

Secret Forty-Eight
CUPID

The picture of a cute little pudgy fellow with bow in hand and a huge pink heart in his sights is famous the world over. This adorable chap is affectionately called Cupid.

Cupid is a caricature of all the wonderful experiences shared by lovers everywhere. He is venerated in rhyme and verse; both author and poets proclaim his mystical prowess. Cupid holds the entire nation spellbound for one day each year. Valentine's Day is celebrated in honor of all who have been pricked by his arrows of love.

Cupid's effect on the human heart can be magical. He can possess your imagination and enliven your soul in spite of past heartaches and disappointments.

Although millions have failed at marriage and numerous other relationships, Cupid continues to prowl the dark corridors of their mind. Somehow they intuitively know they were never loved, or never truly loved another.

Not everyone can confess to feeling another chance at love is possible. Those who have experienced divorce or the loss of a relationship may not be inclined to take a second chance on love. They swear they will never fall in love again. But their denial is only a veiled form of fear. If you could see into their hearts, you would notice a yearning for one more taste of love's sweet nectar. Those who say they will never fall for love a second time would, if they had the opportunity. What they really mean is they don't want to *lose* at love again.

Love isn't about losing; it's about winning. Life is about winning and losing. Don't confuse life with love because if you lost at love, you have really only lived. A decision to refrain from trying your luck at love again won't spare you from Cupid's darts.

Karen, a recent acquaintance of mine, married at an early age and her heart was broken by the pain of divorce. The experience left her with a bitter attitude toward men and a negative outlook on life. She was determined never to fall in love again.

With her defenses in place, Karen immersed herself in her career, spending 50 to 60 hours a week at work. This went on for several years as Karen secretly harbored resentment in heart for the way her marriage ended. She privately slandered her friends who were in relationships.

Karen's job was now her life and nothing else mattered until one December she decided to attend her employer's Christmas party.

While enjoying the party with co-workers, a friend of Karen's boss asked her to dance and she accepted. One dance led to another and before the night was over, Karen felt something she had never felt before. Although she couldn't quite describe it, the feeling intrigued her.

Much to Karen's surprise, the boss's friend called the next weekend and asked her for a date. She accepted without thinking. As the months passed, they continued to see each other.

Karen's new friend was older than her ex-husband and he had experienced divorce too. Karen confided to relatives that she was happy for the first time in her life, but she didn't know why.

Karen and her friend continued dating for nearly a year, then he proposed. In the blink of an eye, Karen accepted and a year later they were married. Cupid had struck again. Karen had taken an arrow straight to the heart.

Nancy also experienced the pain of a broken heart. Her husband ran off with a girlfriend and she was devastated.

Deeply depressed, Nancy began isolating from friends and snubbing co-workers. She reasoned that being alone was safer than running the risk of being hurt again.

Nancy's decision to isolate from the rest of the world seemed irreversible until one Sunday morning when she ventured to church with a neighbor. The two of them were seated in a pew in front of an unassuming young man. Nancy's neighbor knew him. At the close of service Nancy's neighbor greeted the young man. She introduced him to Nancy. Without warning, Nancy felt something magical. Cupid had struck again. His arrows of love penetrated Nancy's unprotected heart.

In Nancy's own words, "One thing led to another and, well you know, we fell in love and got married."

That was two years ago. Today they are happily married and expecting their first child.

You too can love again if the love you find is real. Notice, I said "real." Real means true, genuine, authentic love—not an imitation, counterfeit, or imposter of love. These last are negative aspects of life.

If you confused the negative events of life with love and are afraid you can never love again, don't worry. When you least expect it, love will find you. You may fall in love with the next person you meet. It could happen in the supermarket, a PTA meeting, a volunteer group, a political rally, at work or anywhere you happen to be.

Be aware of the secrets of love and marriage so you will recognize genuine love when it appears.

Secret Forty-Nine
THE ULTIMATE GOAL

What is the ultimate goal? The question requires a two-part answer: A satisfactory relationship and the privilege of self-expression through a labor of love.

In a practical sense, you achieve the ultimate goal when you experience intimacy with another and embark on a meaningful career that captivates your imagination and inspire you to creativity. These two ideals, love and work, shape your identity and lend meaning to your existence.

In Part I, The Perfect Principles of Love & Marriage, you learned about the power of intimacy, the importance of feeling secure, how a decision can ensure that love remains long after the emotion fades, and much, much more.

In Part II, The Painful Problems of Love & Marriage, you were made aware of difficulties caused by in-laws, addictions, money problems, fear and other issues that prevent you from achieving a successful relationship or marriage.

In Part III, The Patient Practice of Love & Marriage, you discovered the power of forgiveness and the importance of owning your feelings, how to get your needs met, and other practical solutions to love's painful problems.

In light of all that you now know, it should be no surprise that here, in the final secret, a satisfactory relationship is identified as part one of your ultimate goal. Can you actually achieve such a lofty ideal? The answer is yes! The secret is to stay away from negativity and develop a positive mental attitude.

Negativity is dangerous because people have difficulty envisioning themselves in a successful relationship or marriage. They think that they can't have what other people have. Unfortunately, when they say they "cannot" they really mean they "will not." They make this choice because they are afraid of failing.

The fear of failure disguises itself as. "It's too difficult." "That is the way I am." "I'm too set in my ways." "There is no use in trying. I can't." And so on.

The fear of failure stops most couples from reaching the highest pinnacle of success in their relationship or marriage. They settle for less, all the while secretly bemoaning the fact they don't have more.

Pause and think about where the fear of failure emanates from. The famous inspirational writer, Napoleon Hill, believed that all of us have at least two prominent natures. One is a negative personality that resides in an atmosphere of doubt, fear, poverty, and ill health.

The negative self expects failure and is seldom disappointed. It dwells on the unpleasant circumstances of life which you desperately want to refuse, but seem obliged to accept. It sends out negative messages that start with "I can't," lead to "What's the use?" and end in "I knew it couldn't happen for me."

You may be very familiar with the negative side of your nature and will do almost anything to avoid hearing, "I told you so,"—the final blow delivered by the negative self.

A second part of everyone's personality is more hopeful. Mr. Hill saw what he called the "other self," or positive side of persona. It thinks in affirmative terms of success, sound health, wealth, friendship, personal achievement, creative vision, service to others and unfailing love. This self is your spiritual side. It brings into existence every wonderful benefit that you can imagine and believe in—including a loving relationship and a contented marriage.

Too many people have had their positive self beaten

down and intimidated into a passive, submissive role by the negative side of their personality. Their positive self is weakened to the point that it is only a faint voice that calls from somewhere deep within. How can you activate it?

Activating the positive you is as simple as turning off the defeatist messages sent your way by the negative self by flipping the switch on your "mental headset." You can flip the switch by reading affirmations, self-help books, devotionals, and other positive, reaffirming works.

During the next thirty days, read all of the affirmations that you find helpful. Select several that are especially meaningful. Reread them three times a day for two weeks. It is amazing what this can do to reset your "mental headset." You will find you have become a positive person—one who believes they can have a satisfying relationship. Above all, the secret to achieving this most cherished objective is believing that you can.

This brings us to the second important part of our ultimate goal—a labor of love.

Your dilemma, no matter who you are, is to find your true place in life. Find it and you will find contentment. The secret is to find your role with your spouse so that both of you can know the joy of living your life's purpose together.

You have probably heard a negative voice inside saying, "I'm just a plain, ordinary person with no special talents, skills or abilities." Or "I'm just a housewife. I don't have a college degree or an expertise for leverage. How can there be something wonderfully fulfilling awaiting me?"

An answer is in the sayings of the renowned mystic, Emmett Fox. He said, "Already in your life, somewhere along the way, God Himself has whispered into your heart the very thing, whatever it is, that He wants you to be, and to do, and to have. And that thing is nothing less than your heart's desire."

Mr. Fox goes on to say, "The most secret desire that resides deep within your heart, the thing you scarcely ever look at, or think about, the thing you wouldn't dare tell anyone of, because it seems too far fetched in your mind, is the very thing that God is desiring for you to be and do for Him."

You can have the desires of your heart. Begin by owning it. Write out your desires and place what you write where you can see it every day. Next, identify all the benefits associated with your desire and establish a plan and a timetable for attaining it. Speak to yourself in positive affirmations that build an unwavering faith in your abilities. Most importantly, get them into action. Desires and planning without works are useless.

When obstacles confront you, stay active. Look for alternative pathways to your goal. Persistent action equals faith. This is the secret to experiencing the personal satisfaction you may be missing. It's the only way to realize your dream.

Norman Vincent Peale said, "A dream vividly imagined. A goal tenaciously pursued. A faith that God will help you with a worthy ambition. An unshakable determination to work and work and keep working. These are all the keys that open the door to the power available to help you achieve your heart's desire."

When you and your partner achieve it together, you will have attained part two of the ultimate goal. I urge you to pursue both parts of the ultimate goal. You deserve the best.

THE END

BOOK LIST

Bradshaw, John. *Creating Love*. New York: Bantam Books, 1992.

Bradshaw, John. *Home Coming: Reclaiming and Championing Your Inner Child*. New York: Bantam Books, 1992.

Covey, Stephen. *The 7 Habits of Highly Effective People*. New York: Simon & Schuster, 1989.

Covey, Stephen. *The 7 Habits of Highly Effective Families*. New York: Golden Books, 1997

Dobson, James. *Love Must be Tough: Straight Talk, What Men Should Know; What Women Need to Understand*. Nashville, TN: Word Books, 1996.

Fox, Emmet. *Find and Use Your Inner Power*. San Francisco, CA: Harper Collins, 1992.

*LaBorde, Mason Hope. *Trick or Treatment: Getting the Most from Psychotherapy*. Ventura, CA: Newjoy Press, 2001.

Nakken, Craig. *The Addictive Personality*. New York: MJF Books, 1996

*Ramsey, Robert. *Relapse Traps: How to Avoid or Escape Them*. Ventura, CA: Newjoy Press, 1998.

*Scott, David. *Living the Authentic Life*. Ventura CA: Newjoy Press, 1999.

Splinter, John P. *The Complete Divorce Recovery Handbook*. Grand Rapids, MI: Zondervan Publishing House, 1992.

Twerski, Abraham J. M.D. *Addictive Thinking*. New York: MJF Books, 1997.

Williamson, Marianne. *A Return to Love: Reflections of a Course in Miracles.*New York: Harper Collins, 1994.

* Use the order form on the last page of this book to order Newjoy Press books or buy them at your book store and on Amazon.com.

INDEX

205

Order Form

Please send me the following books:

#	BOOK TITLE	Price	Total
	NEWJOY PRESS CATALOG	**FREE**	
	Postage & Handling Each book $1.80 Each additional book add 35 cents Orders of 10 or more books invoiced separately. Priority , UPS, Express mail - extra fee	Subtotal	
		*Tax	
		P&H	
		TOTAL	

California residents pay 7.25% sales tax

√ **Mail this form with check or credit card number**
√ **Call: 800-876-1373**
√ **Fax: 805-984-0503**

Card No.___ __ __ __ __ __ __ __ __ __ __ __ __ __ __ __

Signature_____Exp. Date_____
□ Visa   □ MasterCard   □ American Express   □ Check

Please print clearly

Name: _____

Address_____

City, State, Zip _____

Phone (_____)_____

Newjoy Press, P.O. Box 3437, Ventura, CA 93006

Thank you for your order

Guarantee

If, for any reason, you are not satisfied with
your purchase, simply return it and your
money will be refunded.